australian jewellery topos

talking about place with eighteen contemporary australian jewellers

australian jewellery topos
talking about place

talking about place with eighteen contemporary australian jewellers

edited by robert baines, nicole polentas and melissa Miller

australian scholarly publishing

First published 2010 by
Australian Scholarly Publishing Pty Ltd
7 Little Lothian Street North
North Melbourne Victoria 3051
tel: 03 9329 6963 fax: 03 9329 5452
email: aspic@ozemail.com.au web: www.scholarly.info

ISBN: 978-1-921875-05-2

Designed by Barry Robertson, D I N E R G Y
Photography by Jeremy Dillon

contents

essays   6

the art of migration through contemporary jewellery, by elizabeth grierson   6

intelligent jewellery spaces, by robert baines   12

the artists   19

katherine brunacci   20

robert baines   22

elfrun lach   24

anita van doorn   26

dougal haslem   28

julie Mitchell   30

karla way   32

kirsten haydon   34

lucy hearn   36

mel miller   38

natalia milosz-piekarska   40

nicholas bastin   42

nina oikawa   44

penelope joy pollard   46

renee ugazio   48

linda hughes   50

christopher earl milbourne   52

nicole polentas   54

artists' biographies   57

editors & authors   80

the art of migration through contemporary jewellery

elizabeth grierson

The crafting of objects or artefacts presents an innovative way to talk about place. Artefacts carry the imprint of place; they suggest, echo, trace and design our ideas of place. Artefacts can act as a form of knowledge generation about the media and technologies engaged and also about the referential places that are connected in some way, be they conceptual or material, to the making and presentation processes.

This chapter presents some thoughts about the connections of jewellery and place. It considers place through the Greek origins and then looks at how both artists and viewers are transported to different places of meaning through processes of migration of ideas, exhibitions, viewer perceptions and interpretations, and more. The discussion traces the metaphor of the bird to consider ideas of migration and movement, and the potential for revisiting habitual interpretations and making new discoveries. Contemporary jewellery is the bearer of meaning and potential through which these ideas can be expressed, encapsulated and disseminated.

Origins and extensions of place

If we trace an etymological origin of place we find it comes from the Greek, Topos, "of place", and we quickly see the reference to geographic terms like topography and topology. But if we take the term topos into a wider domain of cross disciplinary practice we can easily enter the multi-layered potential of art, craft and design as a way of investing other disciplines with renewed vigour. Craft design through the art of jewellery opens our minds to the potential of crossing boundaries through innovative practices of making, and thereby the possibilities of travelling with ideas and creative potentials to faraway places in both the mind and body. In this sense we open diverse references to historical and contemporary place, personal and public place, social and cultural place, imaginative and actual place, as topos takes on a wider meaning.

We could take this idea even further and say that makers of contemporary jewellery orchestrate the viewers' perceptions and interpretation of the world through psychological and emotional space as well as embodied and cognitive place. There is no doubt that objects and artefacts carry embodied imprints and covert identifications with place, time and circumstance, and they carry us, the viewers and users, along with them. In researching these domains we can consider what these embodied imprints may be, and how they reference elements of place-making.

Tracing the theme of *topos*, place, we can identify four broad areas of attention that can give focus for creative practitioners, viewers and users, as they open spaces for dialogic exchange and reflective analysis in their movements, traces and place-making engagements. These include Topos of remnant and reject materials; Topos of private and personal place; Topos of public place; Topos of historical and cultural locations.

In and through each of these there is a place-making process at work. Not only is there the relation of materials and physical spaces at work here, but there is also a sense of imagination and memory, identity and history, and the layering of sensory awareness of self and world, and finding ways to make sense of the places in which we find ourselves, and to be responsive to revelations at new destinations.

Posing questions and seeking answers: the metaphor of the bird

We could ask how the personal and public artefact identifies and makes meaning of the of the place, beyond its formal objecthood. Furthermore, how do artist-designers, and user-viewers activate personal and public narratives in the making of artefacts to convey changes of habitat? How do we relate to place through objects? Is it possible that the personal and public artefact can assist us to identify and make meaning of place? And if this is so, then what can the designed and crafted object carry, suggest, expose or reveal at those new places?

As we work towards answers to these questions we might turn to the metaphor of 'the bird' as a narrative device. Let us consider for a moment the patterns of bird movements across the globe. They have their imprints; they follow their instinctual drives; they gather and nest together. We can find an analogy here. As many species of birds migrate so do ideas; they move, spread, multiply, cluster. This juxtaposition evokes an expression of independence and adaptability in the movement of ideas and identification with topos in context of building diverse layers of cultural habitat, of creative communities, knowledge and environmental cultures. The artists' explorations of materials have the potential to migrate ideas that take people to another place in geography, time, memory or imagination. Through this imminent potential for translocation we find a range of sensory affects. The relationships between birds and humankind have long been full of complexities, evoking fear and vision, freedom and fantasy, association and dissociation.

The bird is considered as a measure of resilience to environmental change (Furness & Greeenwood, 1993); and through the action of flight the bird has also long been used as an allegory of independence, mobility and the human soul (Werness, 2003, p. 44). Via the metaphor of the bird and migration we can addresses aspects of creativity, independence, mobility, adaptability and identity through the work of artists individually and in groups. It is connectivity, as well as fragmentation, that tends to invigorate our understanding of the way the crafted object or artefact takes its place in the multi-layered cultural settings of its making and its location. Flight, the common feature of most bird species is a way to focus on our own relationships with spatiality; a way to reflect on our own repeating habitats, our own migrations, our place-making attitudes and the role of objects and artefacts within these journeys. Many bird species travel quickly over long distances, up to thousands of kilometres, if necessary crossing seas, deserts or inhospitable areas. Birds can occupy widely separated areas at different seasons, returning repeatedly to the same localities from year to year, and adopting an itinerant lifestyle of a kind not open to less mobile creatures (Newton, 2008, p. 1). Birds are resilient and enduring, and as with artists they carry the imprint of their surroundings and locations as they migrate from place to place. Through these processes in jewellery topos the potential of crafted objects is revealed through aesthetic and epistemological identifications with place.

Widening epistemological and ontological boundaries

The personal and public artefact is epistemological in that it works as a responsive knowledge-generating and knowledge-carrying site. The object therefore becomes part of the viewer's world as much as the maker's world of ontology to provoke a new understanding of relationships. This brings the small crafted object or artefact out of its protected domain of individual art form somewhat detached from the exigencies of social and cultural living, as

was the modernist tradition of art, and activates it beyond a self-enclosed and self-referential environment. The thematic idea of the bird offers an innovative approach to the making of artefact with a powerful form of metaphor for the dialogic methods of creative exchange that are involved. Thus by talking about place and how the crafted objects or artefacts relate to the changing world of local differences and conditions, in context of a globalised world of fast exchange of capital and ideas, we can focus on the relational aspect of object and place as a primary concern. We can also focus on what kinds of ontological changes can occur in makers and viewers when the object reaches its destination.

It is the migration of ideas and their reference to place through the personal and public artefact that is at the core of our interest when we speak of contemporary jewellery, with objects embodying the potential to act as carriers of migrating ideas with public and private, epistemological and ontological references. The metaphor of the bird is a conceptual connection that provides creative scope for innovation and imagination, inviting "a sensory and active participation" (Waterlow, 1997, p. 5). Imaginative and poetic, the connection between bird, object and place is evoking an expression of independence and adaptability in the migration and materialisation of ideas though the movements of contemporary jewellery as a design motif, a cultural way of working, a creative potential for the activation of memory, and a means of relating to self and the world. In this sense contemporary jewellery has an indexical presence that evokes a way of being present to something, one knows not what. The mystery remains.

Belief patterns and creative agency

One of the constant factors of cultural habitation is that human beings wear adornments and accoutrements, carry personal objects and artefacts from place to place, identify with and consume designed and functional objects in homes or transit. Schelereth (1988) states that "objects made or modified by humans, consciously or unconsciously, directly or indirectly, reflect the belief patterns of individuals who made, commissioned, purchased, or used them, and, by extension, the belief pattern of the larger society of which we are part". Thus we are starting from the perspective that personal and public objects or artefacts have a capacity to reflect or convey something deeply felt or personally understood; they also have the capacity to prompt or promote a relationship between self and topos, and the potential exists to do this in multiple ways – personal, material, aesthetic, spatial, locational, as well as social, cultural, historical, psychological, technological, economic and political. I am suggesting that there is a process of activation at work in and through contemporary jewellery, and that the artist-designer working in this field is an artful practitioner who performs more than a mere technological feat of design. They position the migratory potential of ideas and meanings in the crafted object or artefact in a quest for further understanding and analysis of our relationships to place.

If we put crafted objects or artefacts to the test of scrutiny and analysis focusing on the "constituency and intellectual make-up of craft" (Greenhalgh, 1997, p. 47), we will discover more about ourselves and our world in the process. Investigating how the artefact mediates between self and place, we can distinguish five categories of creative agency in the artful practices engaged in jewellery topos. There is, (1) the artist who is the designer or maker of the object or artefact; and (2), the viewers, consumers, commentators, collectors, writers of artefact, who are active makers of meaning through diverse perspectives; and (3), there is the place or setting in which the object or artefact is situated and the knowledge it reveals or embeds; (4) there are the artefacts' material, technological, and iconographical components, and evidence of meanings they carry; and finally, (5) relations between the above components. These categories provide us with a way of thinking around the artefact as the agent of cultural habitation. A gathering is occurring in the processes of world-making.

Migrations and safe landings

The creative agency gives impetus to the making of artefact, yet there is something more at work when one considers the way meanings and references can be carried through time and across space, from one epoch to another, one location to another. A brooch from fifteenth century Europe might reappear in a redesigned form in twenty-first century Australia. A greenstone tiki formation from Aotearoa New Zealand might reappear in another cultural habitat with echoes of the origin overlaid by new possibilities of meaning. However with the trans-historical and trans-locational migrations of these artefacts the artist-designers, and the viewer-users, will exercise their own creative agency to revise and renew the references according to the conditions of topos that are available to them.

Following the migration of jewellery designs and the movement of artists across the globe we can map flight paths and safe landings and trace the way artefact moves and new meanings are created. In 2008 jewellery by Cottrell, Hayden, Bastin and Baines migrated to Cagnes-sur-Mer in southern France. Their jewellery from Australia had landed in a Medieval hill town, there to rest a while and be available for diverse conjunctions of time, history, memory, culture, language and aesthetics. Similarly in 2010 Treasure Room Australia brought the best of Australian jewellery to Munich, Germany – another migration, another conjunction, another self and place mediation.

Today's migration of jewellery topos to Gallery Loupe in Montclair, New Jersey, USA, has its precedent at Galerie Marzee in Nijmegan in the Netherlands in 2009, when young artist-designers could immerse their works in a European culture with references to Australia in the way the pieces were conceptualised, constructed and exhibited, but where new meanings were created in the minds of European viewers. Each of these places holds its particular characteristics, and each jewellery piece and collection migrates the dispositions of its makers and viewers to meet and settle in the new cultural habitat. Like flocks of birds the migrations ensure the life of these jewellery pieces and ways of working. Migrations give the birds life. Similarly through the international exhibiting opportunities these jewellery makers feed their creative horizons as they envisage new worlds.

Predictive thinkers

There is a responsibility resting on the shoulders of the educators whose practices support and inspire the artists and designers of tomorrow. The field of contemporary jewellery needs the courage and focus of educators and supporters who believe in what the artists do, and who enable them to work innovatively with materials and ideas to enter and invent new habitats. In this sense jewellery artists and designers who travel in the mind or physically to absorb other places, other times and other memories, and whose works may travel the globe, reveal our predictive thinkers of the future. They are the ones who deliver new ideas and change the way people think. These thoughts in a recent publication express the belief that artists are the agent provocateurs of the future. We need them to open our horizons to possibilities of further migrations and inventions.

"The global economy needs predictive thinkers, those who can question, reflect, and take risks to enunciate new and possible futures. Artful artists are trained to take these risks. Working as creative entrepreneurs and transformative practitioners, artful artists can see, imagine, predict and take their place in the worlds of innovation, enterprise and productive labour. In the realms of transdisciplinary knowledge, artful art as a way of designing offers new ways of seeing beyond sight, knowing beyond the already known, and imagining the possible (Grierson, 2010, p. 128)."

The artists, whose ideas are presented here and whose works have migrated previously to other places, open ideas of topos to diverse references for our examination and wonder. They are the artful artists of the future. With a globalised sense and a creative sensibility beyond any quotidian horizons, these artists put the work of art to work as they open possibilities of topos in a contemporary world of change. In so doing they show how place can be identified through the personal and public artefact;

they advance the creative arts as a way of thinking through their design practice; and they take the potential of contemporary jewellery beyond the already-thought and into new forms of imaginative invention with the amalgamation of technë and poetics, memory and meaning, innovation and imagination.

Elizabeth Grierson, PhD, FRSA, is Professor of Art and Philosophy, and Head of the School of Art at RMIT University, Melbourne, Australia. Leading the Intervention through Art research program in Design Research Institute she links research in art, object, and place and space. Elizabeth is co-author of Creative Arts Research: Narratives of Methodologies and Practices (Sense Publishers, Rotterdam, 2009); and A Skilled Hand and Cultivated Mind: A Guide to the Architecture and Art of RMIT University (RMIT Press, 2008). She is co-editor of Thinking through Practice: Art as Research in the Academy (RMIT Press, 2007); and The Arts in Education: Critical perspectives from Aotearoa New Zealand (Dunmore Press, 2003). Published in a range of journals, she is also Executive Editor of ACCESS:Critical Perspectives on Communication, Cultural and Policy Studies.

References

Furness, R.W. & Greeenwood, J.J. D. (Eds.) (1993). Birds as Monitors of Environmental Change. London: Chapman & Hill.

Greenhalgh, P. (1997). The History of Craft. In P. Dormer (Ed.) The Culture of Craft (pp. 20-52). Manchester & New York: Manchester Metropolitan University Press.

Grierson, E. (2010). Artful Art as an Interventionist Strategy in Transdisciplinary Design. In T. Cutler (Ed.) Designing Solutions to Wicked Problems: A Manifesto for Transdisciplinary Research and Design (pp. 127-128). RMIT Design Research Institute. Melbourne: RMIT University Press.

Newton, I. (2008). The Migration Ecology of Birds. London: Academic Press.

Schelereth, T.J. (1988). Cultural History ad Material Culture: Everyday Life, Landscapes, Museums. Ann Arbor USA: UMI Research Press.

Waterlow, N. (1997). Preface. In S. Rowley (Curator and Ed.) The Somatic Object (p. 5). Sydney: Ivan Dougherty Gallery.

Werness, H.B. (2003). The Continuum Encyclopedia of Animal Symbolism in Art. London: Continuum International Publishing Group.

intelligent jewellery spaces

robert baines

Jewellery manufacture requires a place or site. Within the domain of technë, process (technology, making) there are workstations where charcoal hearths might be found but in more contemporary times, jewellery making activities centre around electric kilns, micro torches and laser welders. Fabrication and assembly has been located on floors, doorsteps, tables, cut out benches and even a comfortable bed in front of the television. The place of material manipulation leading to the made object abounds from a knowledge base –another place where the maker draws on knowledge conscious practices or empowered from tacit knowledge spaces. "Place is perceived as in some sense 'bounded', particularly in relation to the seemingly endless extension of space"(Dean & Millar, 2005)

The jewellery place can be a location for files, fluxes and solders with shelves of hand tools, primary resource materials, found and collected objects and earlier 'unhappy' works. It's the location for sounds and smells intrinsically connected to processes of jewellery manufacture. Drawings prescribing jewellery forms can litter the space, fixed to the wall or lay stacked in a pile of accompanying dormant jewellery designs.

Industry is implicit in the spectacle of these jewellery making spaces, but what is it that challenges and entices the artist jeweller to enter into this seemingly one dimensional spatial environment of manufacture? Are there other jewellery places and spaces? "Place is not a one dimensional notion; it is much more than a physical location. Places are both material and mental constructions; they are locations or sites, as well as personal, intangible and mythical webs of associations and memories"(den Besten, 2006).

There is the poësis (poetics of making) which requires jewellery making places without pre-emptive conclusions. Historically and in contemporary practice jewellery has been a bearer of cultural and historical meaning and memory. In particular it has been concerned with the relations of those meanings with the personal and urban settings, acting as a way of defining or interpreting topos (which means 'of place', Greek). The Australian jewellers in this exhibition are RMIT Gold and Silversmithing post graduates or alumni and their concern for their research outputs to travel to Gallery Loupe, Montclair USA is to recognise and explore the ways the jewellery artefact opens our engagement with, and understanding of the personal and external places we inhabit. The jewellers engage with topos and they consider its multi-layered potential as historical and contemporary place, personal and public place, time and circumstance.

Making personal jewellery artefact is a multi material trans disciplinary practice and the research approach to topos, place, identifies four broad areas of attention providing design practice, and dialogic exchange: (1) Topos of remnant, reject industrial materials, found and collected residue materials and objects, remnant domestic and public detritus. (2)Topos of private and personal place, intimate locations, human body, internal architectural spaces, domestic applications and circumstances. (3)Topos of public place, streetscapes, external spaces and community locations. (4) Topos of historical and cultural locations, personal histories and poetries.

These Australian jewellery researchers making artefact see mind and body as topos. What is the significance of designing knowledge through these different (polymath) systems?

Topology chosen by Renee Ugazio in her work De-phile is the process of making- the technë. She posits that almost every act of jewellery making requires the extraction process of the file and this is a repetitive abrasive activity. De-phile transforms our understanding of a file, a tool by reconfiguring and transcendence follows from the workshop to the sensitive site on the body. The file is redirected and becomes decoration of and for place, the body.

The Australian art jewellers exhibiting at Montclair are building personal artefact empowered with embodied imprints and covert identity. Karla Way conjures objects from some past and fictitious place – or is it? Entropy abounds amidst objects in a state of ruin or is it some primordial process of osmosis? Things are in flux in the unlikely conjoin of chaos and progress

Jewellery conveys streams of human identity and presence as well as external settings such as urban spaces and topos takes on a broader significance as place itself becomes an expanded notion. Julie Mitchell contemplates the devotional object as the outcome of inner observation and thinking, and this becomes a vehicle to enhance qualities of awareness and equanimity. The materials of paper and thread and the repetitive process of assembly of the devotional object are chosen to reflect this internal meditative experience.

How can crafting jewellery artefact embody imprints and covert identifications with place, time and circumstance and be an innovative way to tell us about place? Is the place of robotics topos for Dougal Haslem or is this too simplistic? It is the robotics, that technë for creating the poësis in his 'elephant with an umbrella subject' he has been researching.

 The jewellery research asks: How does the personal artefact identify and make meaning of the location in which it is made, situated, used, viewed and transferred, beyond its self-referential nature? Nicole Polentas visiting her family's origins on the island of Crete confronts social cultural history through artefact, photographs and maps. These become available iconography in her jewellery assemblages.

What can the designed and crafted object carry, expose or reveal? Julie Mitchell manipulates her chosen material, paper and thread in a repetitive configuration to transcend the simplicity of their nature. In her making, these pieces become a living expression of the moment, as it is in contemplation and by this experience the viewer is given insight into the meditative

place or condition.

There is in these studio jewellery practices revelation of artefact making and analysis acting as a form of knowledge generation through innovative practices. Mel Miller transforms landscapes, both real and imagined, into jewellery objects that act as metaphors for memory. Conditions of hard and soft become metaphor for past and present. These renderings inhabit wearable jewellery and functional/non functional objects and when configured into series the time span alters memory. This is the topography of memory: a landscape of inversion and invention, embellishment and exaggeration. It is a topos that exists in the moment of interaction when past and present collide in a shower of memory.

The jewellers are locating cultural and historical memory via practice based design processes. Nicole Polentas examines a transcultural evolution between East and West, constructing narratives of cultural identity. The objects are constructed within the framework of the Karagiozis character drawing on the cultural identities explored in the urban theatre to negotiate and define boundaries and sense of place within the Cretan community. Nick Bastin considers the possible link between jewellery and the Japanese action figure and the potential to create new narratives in miniature object.

 How do we design, discover and identify topos and materiality of our lives in the current era? Natalia Milosz-Piekarska's work lies within the blurred divisive lines between object and subject. The animist notion that inanimate objects can be imbued with incarnation. This is intriguing as she explores ideas of totemism, fetishism and the 'spirit' within objects. Natalia's work triggers a sense of nostalgia and mythology as she injects her pieces with fragments of the familiar and the mysterious. There is an investigation of materials and processes and how they can become signage of place and time.

Some times jewellers revisit locations of the past. Robert Baines enters the historic domain of Bronze Age linear wire jewellery constructions and invented new forms are revealed. His jewellery objects on another level become a vehicle to declare a political place of a vanishing Australian culture by loading meaning on the colour, 'Forget–me–not-blue'. This play on words connects with the song Hey True Blue by John Williamson (1986) and particularly the line, are you really disappearing, Just another dying race, Hey True Blue…

Why engage in materials to make applications of personal and impersonal objects and their placing in private and public space? Nicholas Bastin finds intrigue in alternate worlds and visits modern mythologies of popular culture, such as the Star Wars film trilogy and the oeuvre of Japanese anime director Hayao Miyazaki. He observes they have all created other worlds that continue a narrative beyond film through the fan idolatry of spawned merchandise.

Penelope Pollard explores peripheries of different genres, cultural styles and social codes, by incorporating and exploring sculptural and painterly processes into her jewellery making practice. The subject investigates evolution of representations of the human face in the Modern and Post Modern period and reconfiguring the meaning of the facial portrait of faces by examining the language of figuration, with the industrial technique of electroforming and fired enamel.

Designing object and placement in geospatial contexts has a multiplicity of possibilities. Linda Hughes reconceptualises the 'cautionary street stripe' and as in historical places it has been regarded as a metonym for danger, exclusion, and as a device used to attract attention. The cautionary stripes are manipulated in shape, colour, texture and pattern transposed to a jewellery scale becoming familiar motifs transposed as jewellery subject.

Placement in another geospatial place is the work of Kirsten Haydon and her fabricating fictitious souvenir of that exotic place, Antarctica. Her jewellery both connects to and explores human experience and place. There is a re-imagining of historical examples of tourist jewellery and personal souvenirs to present further understandings of Antarctica's significance both culturally and environmentally.

Jewellery artefact and its placement in interior architectural space or placed on the body informs cultural topology. How do these jewellery researchers declare the intimate, domestic and public space with artefact/object? Does the intimate object have a domestic cultural role? Lucy Hearn asks the question, "What use is a bowl with holes"? It may not carry much liquid, but how many other things could it not contain? "Tout calice est demeure" every chalice is a dwelling place. (Bachelard, 1994), a dwelling place for the invisible… thoughts, dreams, memories, regrets. The things we all value so highly and yet remain intangible.

Can artefact fulfil a source of comfort in a transient memory and topos? Designers consider their making of artefact a means of dispensing an experience. Designed artefact can transform what may have been an ordinary experience into an interesting and satisfying sensation.

Elfrun Lach has ongoing research into the historic use, depiction and symbolism of coral in connection with making contemporary artefacts. Coral is one of the oldest materials used for human adornment and, because of its difficulty to obtain, has been simulated throughout history by bone, glass, wood, porcelain and plastic. Her investigation of historicity and symbology of coral in the making of contemporary artefact combines topos of historical and cultural locations with topos of found and collected materials and remnant domestic or industrial detritus.

Can the crafted artefact convey a symbol of human presence and in an increasingly dematerialised world embody connections with humanity? Anita Van Doorn pursues an extension of her intimate space of bodily experience, memory and emotion, and articulated through underwater and subconscious landscapes where one experiences and is minutely and wholly part of their shift and flow. Her most recent work is conceptually located within the Estonian word ääremaa, and if it were translated into English, would relate to 'periphery,' although not merely in a geographical sense. The Estonian word ääremaa extends beyond this to encompass the metaphysical, the emotional, the untouchable, a location that exists in language, created by language.

Is this tracing of humanity in the object a primary contrast to the mass-produced industrial designed object? Reinterpreting gem set jewels by Katherine Brunacci is her topos - a place in jewellery history. Jewellery designs sourced from works by jewellers dating from the 1850's to the mid 1900's are reviewed and revisited using techniques developed to emulate precious gems and symbolic motifs. Jewellers/designers such as Bvlgari, Van Cleef and Arpels, and Seaman Schepps, Wiener Werkstatte, and Rene Laliqué are main influences. Such jewellers incorporated precious gems and symbolic of high society sophisticates. Nina Oikawa has investigated how early twentieth century costume jewellery has employed various manmade substances to simulate or substitute for precious gems.

Her jewellery topos brings together the making of plastic gems with inclusions of various kinds and the construction of jewellery using multiple repetitive metal structures and traditional gems and gem setting techniques to create objects which by their scale, colour, and use of unorthodox materials

both reference and subvert historical jewellery, particularly that of the late Middle Ages and Baroque periods.

The various found and constructed objects trapped within resin used to create jewels evoke comparisons with mineralogical features.

Dougal Haslem investigates and discovers topos by dismantling things with miniature mechanical parts - 'just to see how they work'. This has led to the creation of a series of personal objects and jewellery conveying the absurd and mechanical characters, exhausted automatons, and these invite re-animation in the minds of the wearer or viewer.

Whimsical characters are based on two main elements: the application of collected objects creating anthropomorphic and zoomorphic forms, and the indication of movement through the use of visually mechanistic elements. Both are imbued with and evoke a sense of whimsy.

These jewellery makers of artefact engaging in materials declare their making as a means of distributing an expertise. Process is Christopher Earl Milbourne's topos. Specifically it is the nexus between the action of the fire, duration and the chemical condition of the sterling silver alloy. Once the phenomena are understood the joining system is applied in the atmosphere of the fire and the construction process becomes the place.

These Australian jewellers, research the role of the artefact as a bearer of cultural and historical meaning and memory, a carrier of human presence in an increasingly dematerialised world. Tracings of humanity mark the aesthetic presence of object hood in contemporary jewellery works. Each of the jewellers has their own private places for their jewellery investigations but there is another external topos that the jewellery takes them. Recent placings of jewellery topos research have been at Galerie Marzee, Nijmegen the Netherlands 2009 and Ville de Cagnes-sur-Mer, France also in 2009. The eighteen contemporary jewellers now take their jewellery subjects to Gallery Loupe Montclair, New Jersey under the title of Australian Jewellery Topos: Talking about Place.

Robert Baines PhD, is Professor of Art and coordinator of Post Graduate Gold and Silversmithing in the School of Art at RMIT University, Melbourne Australia. His multi-disciplinary research is comprised of three areas: first as an artist goldsmith; second in archaeometallurgy; and third in publishing text and commentary. Robert has received national and international awards and prizes and most recently in these research areas: Senior research scholarship in The Sherman Fairchild Center for Objects Conservation at the Metropolitan Museum of Art in New York (2008) and the Friedrich Becker Preis, Hanau Germany (2008). His work as an exhibiting artist goldsmith for forty years is collected in prestigious public collections in Great Britain, Germany, France, New Zealand, USA and

Australia. Most recent books published are Partyline (RMIT Press 2004) and Bracelet'Java-la-Grande' (Palgrave Macmillan 2006). Treasure room Australia - Schatzkammer Australien, (Australia Scholarly Publishing 2009) and More Amazing Schmuck Stories by Robert Baines (Australia Scholarly Publishing 2009)

References

Bachelard, G., (1969), The Poetics of Space (Jolas, M. Trans.). Boston:Beacon Press

Baines R., (2009) Melbourne Hollow Ware more snakes than you can poke a stick at RMIT University Gold and Silversmithing

Baines, R. (ed.), (2009) Treasure room Australia - Schatzkammer Australien, Melbourne: Australia Scholarly Publishing

Den Besten, L., (2006) Place(s), Making Places, edition 3, Think Tank, a European Initiative for the Applied Arts

Dean, T & Millar, J., (2006) Place, London: Thames and Hudson

Pattison, S., (2007) Seeing things: Deepening relations with visual artefacts. London:SCM Press

the
artists

katherine brunacci

reinterpreting gem set jewels

Topos is a place in history. Designs sourced from works by jewellers dating from the 1850's to the mid 1900's are reviewed and revisited using techniques that I have developed to emulate precious gems and symbolic motifs. Jewellers/designers such as Bvlgari, Van Cleef and Arpels, and Seaman Schepps, Wiener Werkstatte, and Rene Laliqué are main influences. Such jewellers incorporated precious gems and symbolic motifs in their works, and emphasized them, utilizing complex jewellery structures and specific assemblage of material.

The purpose in referencing designs by these jewellers is to reinterpret the gem set jewel and position it into a modern context, creating a new genre with a strong historical reference.

My Double Life 2009
neckpiece
fine silver, sterling silver, opals, enamel
180 x 400 x 20 mm

To My Devine 2009
brooch
fine silver, sterling silver, enamel
150 x 80 x 15 mm

robert baines

hey true blue Topos in this jewellery is historical wire and its contexts in jewellery artifact and this is informing for the building of fine art jewellery.[1] The use of wire to build jewellery structures in art making has direct historic derivations, though at times this may appear quite obscure. The knowledge of ancient and historic wire particularly through 'laboratory reconstruction' has been a profound vantage point to apply in a contemporary context.[2] Networks of multiple combinations of wire manipulations build composite forms and surfaces with the intention to invent new wire systems and linear network placings as strategies to capture space. In this jewellery there is a seeming dismantling of historic formalism, and the application of colour and paint in an almost graffiti approach further extends this.

The *Forget-me-not Blue* neckpiece and brooch visit the political space identified by Australian singer John Williamson (1986), "Are you really disappearing, Just another dying race, Hey True Blue…."

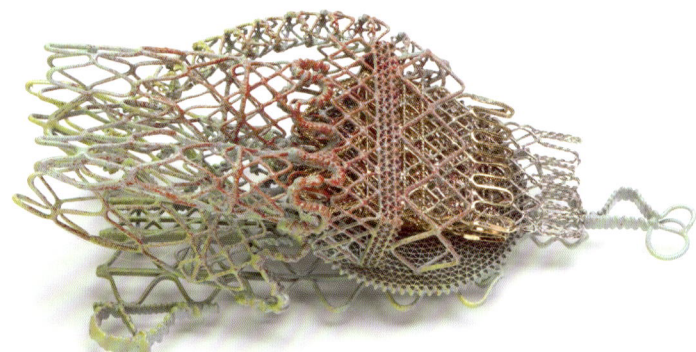

Hey True Blue 2010
brooch
silver, powdercoat, electroplate, paint
73 x 170 x 70 mm

1 For a comprehensive study on ancient and medieval wire manufacture see J. Ogden (1991) 95 – 105, N. Whitfield (1998) 82,83 See also R Baines, 'Technical Decisions in the Gold Cylinders from Praeneste', OAO, 2, (St. Germaine en Laye, 1993).L. Burkhalter, (1993) 5-12. A catalogue of published Etruscan gold disc ear ornaments from the sixth to the fifth century B.C. located in major collections in the United States and Europe. To the list should be added the following: Malibu, J. Paul Getty Museum L.85. AM.72.11.
2 Liesbeth den Besten, Hedendaags Filigrain, Kunstenaarsmateriaal, NL,Winter 06/07, pp.30-33.

Hey True Blue 2010
pendant
silver, powdercoat, electroplate, paint
290 x 178 x 72 mm

elfrun lach

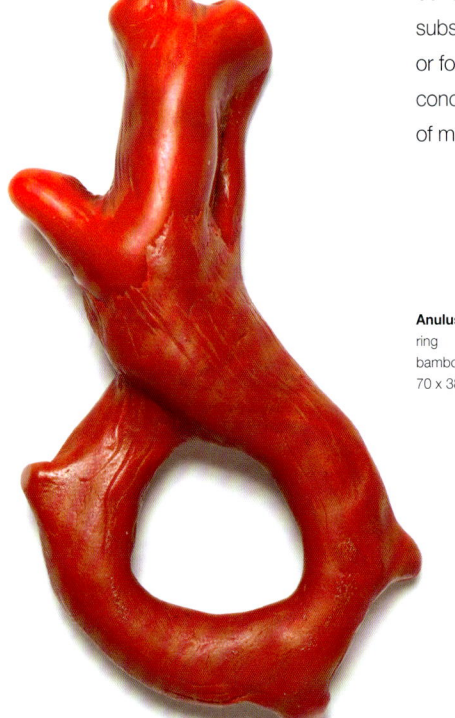

My jewellery topos is the historic use, depiction and symbolism of coral in connection with making contemporary artefacts.

Coral is one of the oldest materials used for human adornment and, because of its difficulty to obtain, has been simulated throughout history by bone, glass, wood, porcelain and plastic. This process of simulation and substitution of materials and the combination of precious and common or found objects is relevant to all my work. I want to generate readings concerning human interaction with the environment and question ethical use of materials and the nature of the real and the represented.

The subject of historicity and symbology of coral in the making of contemporary artefact combines topos of historical and cultural locations with topos of found and collected materials and remnant domestic or industrial detritus.

Anulus Parvus 2008 2008
ring
bamboo coral, polymer clay
70 x 38 x 15 mm

Scarabaeus Rufus 2008
natural twig, enamel paint, wooden beads, found plastic,
silk thread, sterling silver, stainless steel
95 x 50 x 45 mm

anita van doorn

Personal and universal, subconscious and submerged, my work is an extension of my intimate space of bodily experience, memory and emotion, articulated through underwater and subconscious landscapes where one experiences and is minutely and wholly part of their shift and flow.

In the recent work the topos is conceptually located within the Estonian word *ääremaa*, and if it were translated into English, would relate to 'periphery'. This is not merely in a geographical sense. The Estonian word *ääremaa* extends beyond this to encompass the metaphysical, the emotional, the untouchable, a location that exists in language, is created by language.

Within this group of jewellery is the pendant entitled 'Bereft'. It is a term used where something is found to be wanting, lacking, or stripped of usually a non-material asset, also lonely and abandoned. This object is a residual memory of a vessel adrift, or perhaps deposited on the sea floor, flickering and shimmering under or on the surface of the water, the fleeting residue, itself uncatchable as light is uncatchable, of what is now no longer there.

Like the explorers that sailed to the ends of the earth, we sail on the periphery of consciousness, where we see no further than what we can know, and what we know dissipates. Out in the borderlands, where humanity meets loss, and it is surely not safe.

Bereft 2010
pendant
sterling silver
80 x 30 x 20 mm

Urashima's Gift 2008
neckpiece
perspex, opal, digital print,
sterling silver, silk
160 mm dia

dougal haslem

Is an elephant holding an umbrella on a ring an absurd object?

A fascination with dismantling things with miniature mechanical parts 'just to see how they work' has led to the creation of a series of personal objects and jewellery. The pieces are absurd and mechanical characters, exhausted automatons are inviting re-animation by the wearer or viewer.

The whimsical characters are based on two main elements: the application of collected objects creating anthropomorphic and zoomorphic forms, and the indication of movement through the use of visually mechanistic elements. Both have the ability to invoke a sense of curiosity and intrigue in the wearer or viewer, proposing the questions, *Can that move?* or *Can I make it move?* It is important that they will be fun and humorous figures imbued with character and presented in a personal object.

The Elephant and the Umbrella 2008
ring
sterling silver, collected object
90 x 40 x 20 mm

Mutual Friends 2010
brooch pin with stand
sterling silver, copper, collected object
75 x 70 x 30 mm

julie mitchell

The devotional object is the outcome of inner observation and thinking, and its development enhances qualities of awareness and equanimity.

The materials and the repetitive process of assembly are chosen to reflect this internal experience.

Certain materials in a repetitive configuration transcend the simplicity of their nature. In the making, these pieces become a living expression of the moment, as it is in contemplation and by this experience the viewer is given insight into the meditative condition.

I continue to explore the question of excluding certain materials and processes not only from a conceptual base but also in response to the questions of ethical practice. Thinking about the future I wonder how to adapt personally to change and the dilemma that over-consumption, mining and chemical waste present in the production of art objects.

Agghika / A string of garland 2007-2010
paper, cotton thread
20 mm x 5 mm x varied length

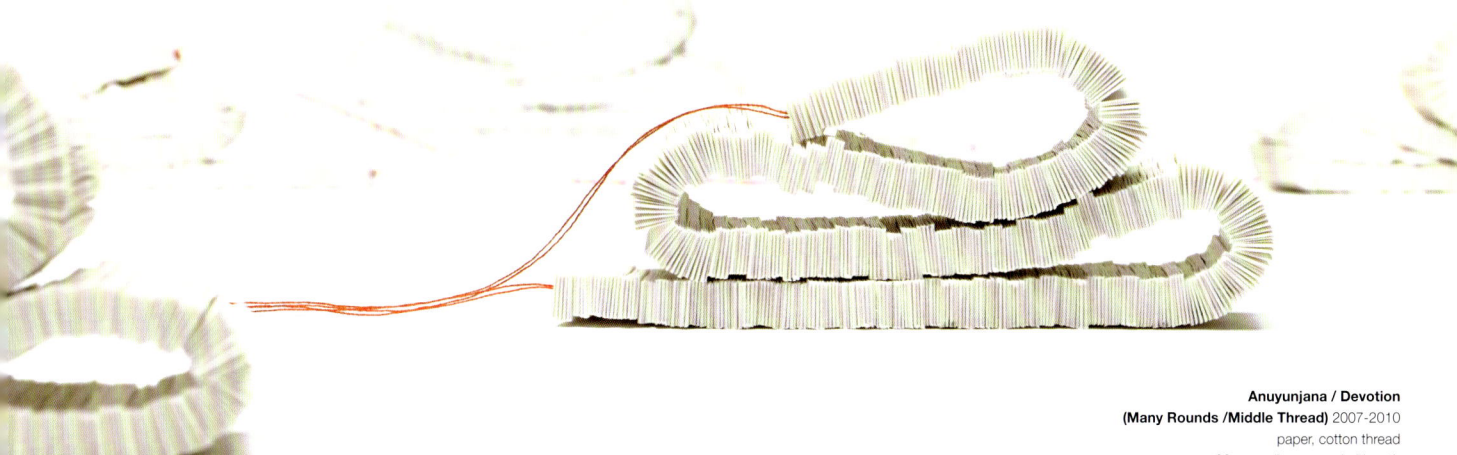

Anuyunjana / Devotion
(Many Rounds /Middle Thread) 2007-2010
paper, cotton thread
20 mm x 5 mm x varied length

karla way

suspended time lines

"Already a fictitious past occupies in our memories the place of another, a past of which we know nothing with certainty – not even that it is false." [3]

These are objects to be suspended, utilitarian vessels to be carried, becoming personal items of adornment. They are from a fictitious landscape that we do not know; the place is fictitious, or is it?

They are in a state of ruin, nature has intruded upon a human made form, and they have become inseparable.[4] There is an entropic force at work, a pull towards a chaos that is metamorphic and evolutionary.[5]

The time line is skewed, prehistory collides with modernity, morphing, like the ambiguity of the materials employed. Things are in flux, chaos and progress.

The place is underneath, below the surface, but which surface?

(Objects to be) Suspended Timelines 3 2008
enclosed vessel to be worn as pendant
perspex, polyurethane resin, sterling silver, silk cord, cotton
118 x 116 x 480 mm

3 Borges, Jorge Luis. Tlon, Uqbar, Orbis Tertius. Labyrinths. King Penguin, 1985. pg 42

4 Hetzler, Florence M. Causality: Ruin Time and Ruins. Leonardo, Vol 21, No1,1988, p51-55

5 Sky, Alison&Smithson, Robert. Entropy Made Visible, Interview with Robert Smithson. Robert Smithson: The Collected Writings, Berkeley: University of California Press, 1996.Berkeley and Los Angeles, California; London, England

(Objects to be) Suspended Timelines 1 2008
suspended vessel with stalactite like growths, to be worn as
pendant
perspex, polyurethane resin, sterling silver, silk cord, cotton
540 x 95 x 58 mm

kirsten haydon

Jewellery topos both connects to and explores human experience and place. I draw on the notion of the souvenir to explore these themes within my work.

Recently my work has concentrated on the experience of the Antarctic landscape, a unique and overwhelming place. Since Antarctica's discovery and exploration both before and during the Heroic Age explorers, expeditioners, artists and writers have attempted to record and visualise Antarctica. Since 2004, when I traveled as a New Zealand Antarctic Arts Fellow, I have been working from my experience of Antarctica and interpreting both personal photographs and re-examining the historic stories, photographs and representations of Antarctica.

My interpretations of Antarctica engage with the viewer through recognizable personal jewellery and souvenir objects. Within my research I explore the use of enameling in contemporary jewellery making by experimenting with processes used in historical souvenirs like micro mosaics and miniatures. I investigate new and innovative ways to interpret these techniques, including the fusing of traditional enamel with reflector beads. Through these investigations I use my findings to re-imagine historical examples of tourist jewellery and personal souvenirs to present further understandings of Antarctica's significance both culturally and environmentally.

Ice Store 2007
brooch
enamel, copper, photo transfer, reflector
beads, silver, steel
80 x 140 x 15 mm

Ice Industry 2009
brooch
enamel, copper, photo transfer, silver, steel
70 x 130 x 15 mm

lucy hearn

Domestic, colour, line, vessel, holes, jewel

What use is a bowl with holes? It may not carry much liquid, but how many other things could it not contain? *"Tout calice est demeure" (every chalice is a dwelling place[6])*, a dwelling place for the invisible… thoughts, dreams, memories, regrets. The things we all value so highly and yet remain intangible.

My personal topos of domestic activities and objects is referenced through my use of form, material and methodology such as ironing (the plastic beads) and baking (firing the enamel).

A quick line drawing manifests as an enamelled vessel, is it a bowl? No. It's a brooch! A wearable bowl. Using these small vessel forms, I conjure a white space which is inhabited by colour and light, it fills the interior with a subtle glow of light. There is a softness of form which conveys human subtleties and variations, inviting personal interaction. Reminiscent of the personal relationships formed with everyday household objects. This one remains not just as a brooch but as a three dimensional line drawing.

White Wing Brooch Pink 2008
copper, enamel, sterling silver, plastic
140 x 55 x 30 mm

6 Cited in The Poetics of Space, p55, Gaston Bachelard, 1994, Beacon Press, Boston

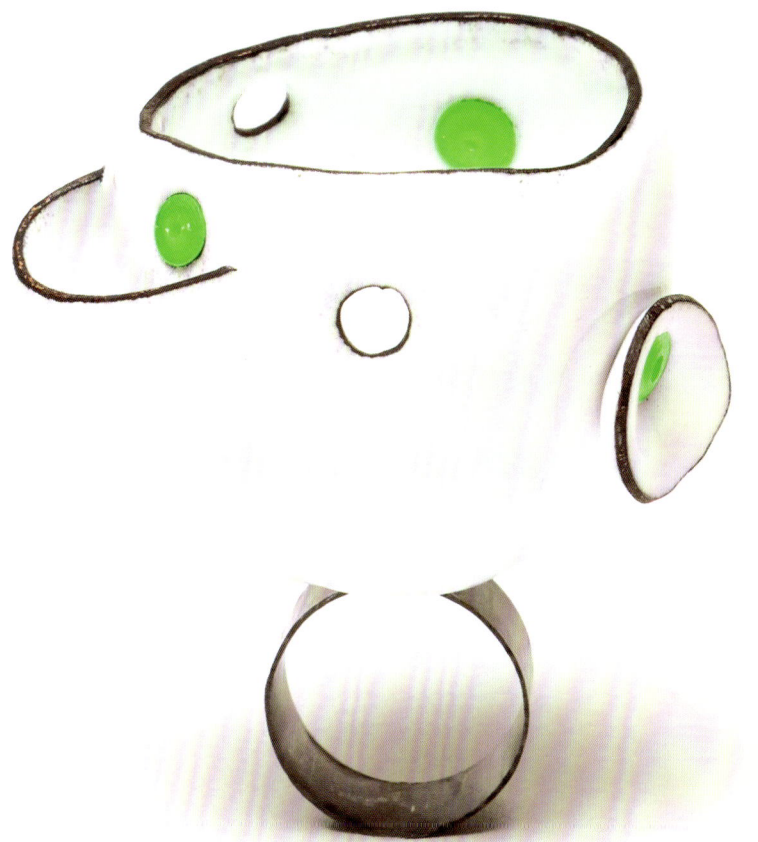

White Ring Green 2007
copper, enamel, sterling silver, plastic
55 x 45 x 40 mm

mel miller

"Memory diminishes original experiences only when we expect them to be duplicated; its transformations can enhance them."[7]

This is a transformation of landscapes, both real and imagined, into jewellery objects that act as metaphors for memory. Through the juxtaposition of hard and soft, past and present forms take shape. Through the interaction between wearable jewellery and the objects it inhabits, the interaction between memory and the events it narrates is revealed. As the objects and jewellery morph into a series, so does memory alter over time.

This is the topography of memory: a landscape of inversion and invention, embellishment and exaggeration. It is a topos that exists in the moment of interaction when past and present collide in a shower of memory. Miniature memory models act as metaphors for a topos based in both place and time. Through the repetition of personal experience and repeated recollections of it, the knowledge of a place over time and affected by varied conditions transforms generic space into personal place.

The ordinary is transformed into the precious: the mundane becomes magical. These works are a celebration of memory's ability to enrich the present by embellishing the past.

Foggy Day in Parkville (Winter, clearing) 2010
brooch
sterling silver, enamel, copper, labradorite,
bouncy balls, felted wool, enamel paint
90 x 80 x 35 mm

7 Lowenthal, D. 1985. *The Past is a Foreign Country*. Cambridge: Cambridge University Press

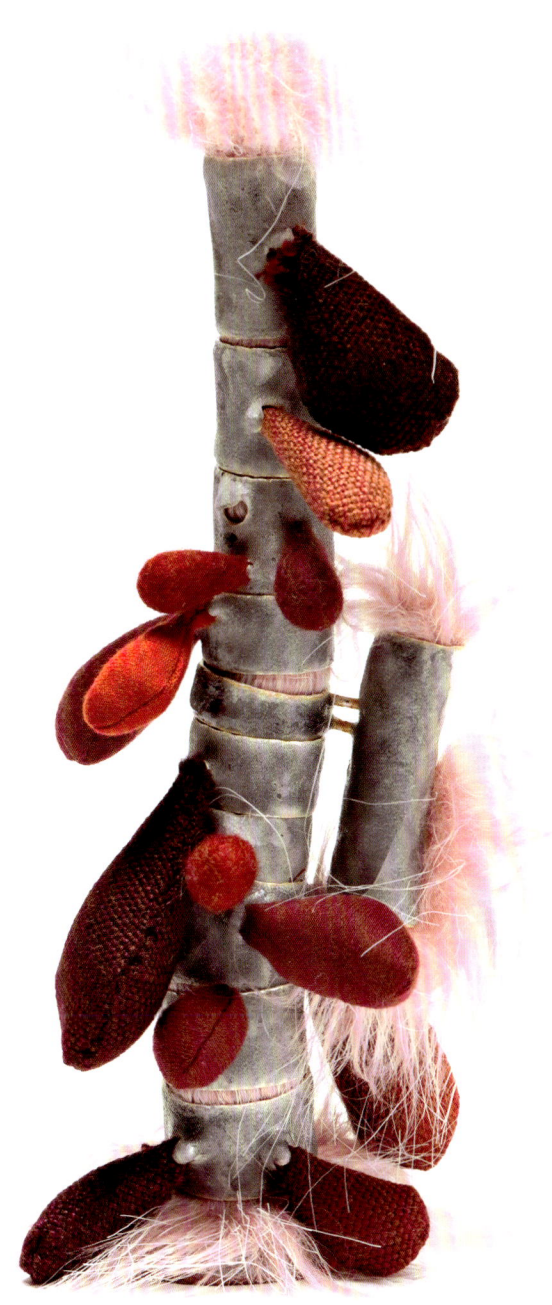

Mnemochronolog 3 2008
Object with removable rings
fine silver, enamel, fabric, polyester, felted wool
190 x 70 x 50 mm

natalia milosz-piekarska

Natalia Milosz-Piekarska's work lies within the blurred divisive lines between object and subject. The animist notion that inanimate objects can be imbued with a spirit, a 'liveness,' is intriguing as she explores ideas of totemism, fetishism and the 'spirit' within objects. Natalia's work triggers a sense of nostalgia and mythology as she injects her pieces with fragments of the familiar and the mysterious.

Working with a vast array of materials, both traditional and unorthodox, such as timber, silver, beading, resin, paint and collected ephemera, Natalia assembles her whimsical treasures with an intuitive and spirited approach.

Natalia's intention is not to recreate or imbue established beliefs into her pieces; rather, she aims to create works that emanate a sense of mystery, reverence and potency. Her topos revolves around creating totemic objects without a prescribed story. The forms, colours and materials used in the works are merely the framework for a story and sprit to unfold. These objects do not reference any particular form of belief rather the structure of belief in itself.

"Myth must be kept alive. The people who can keep it alive are the artists of one kind or another. The function of the artist is the mythologization of the environment and the world."

Joseph Campbell

Cluster 2008
neckpiece
textile, pepper corns, rice, coral, glass beads,
plastic beads, cotton
60 x 100 x 370 mm

Strange Fruit 2010
neckpiece
timber, polyester resin, glass & timber
beads, paint, shark vertebrae, cord
70 x 45 x 40 mm

nicholas bastin

The topos is the possible link between jewellery and the action figure and the potential to create new narratives in miniature. Modern mythologies of popular culture, such as the *Star Wars* film trilogy and the oeuvre of Japanese anime director *Hayao Miyazaki*, have all created other worlds that continue a narrative beyond film through the fan idolatry of spawned merchandise. I am fascinated by these alternate worlds, where a beloved narrative can be 'possessed' through a personal collection and cultivation of the object.

This has lead me to investigate the miniature object fascination in Japan, a culture that is often perceived as encapsulating both the notion of the futuristic and the traditional. Action figures derived from anime and manga narratives, the *gachapon* toy, miniature scenes found in the urban landscape and the small spaces within take-away containers, are all reference points. These are amalgamated into new ambiguous objects that suggest possible origins from a distant parallel land, one that is simultaneously futuristic and ancient.

I employ the notion of plasticity through material and concept. Found materials have been manipulated and renewed and new plastic components have been invented. Plastic urban detritus is almost always present in my work, whether it is real or 'fake'.

The jewellery objects are action figures, spaceships and landing platforms; all miniaturised products of a narrative from an invented utopian world, one that is ever expanding and evolving, but one that is just slightly out of sync with the real world.

Depiction of a Tortoise with Unidentifiable Object 2009
brooch
sterling silver, monel, polyurethane resin, epoxy resin
115 x 85 x 55 mm

Mint Packet #1 (sans background) 2009
brooch
sterling silver, copper, monel, polyurethane resin, epoxy resin
80 x 35 x 30 mm

nina oikawa

Wearable objects are created from my playful imagination using a combination of precious materials and collected materials.

I experiment and search for possibilities in use of various materials. Resin gems are made from the result of my interest in the properties of natural gemstones and set in constructed objects mainly made from silver. One of my interests is to find and create an attractive internal and external space with my methods of resin casting and polishing techniques and to create resin gems. Balance of colours, scale and compositions of units are always considered in the building of my works. Decorative forms are influenced by antique objects such as Victorian, Edwardian, Art Deco and Chinoiserie. *Ikebana* technique is also an influence to determine balance. Each jewellery object is built under the influence of certain types of natural gemstones such as ruby, emerald and opal, which leads me to experiment in many different directions.

Fossil Opal 2010
ring
sterling silver, resin, agate, amethyst, citrine, sapphire,
cubic zirconia, cellophane, nylon mesh
70 x 90 x 90 mm

Fossil Ocean 2010
ring
sterling silver, resin, freshwater pearls, akoya pearl,
sapphire, citrine, amethyst, calcite, leaves
120 x 60 x 60 mm

penelope joy pollard

"The lace curtains on the backs of chairs were painted to look like paper and the paper flowers were painted to look like lace. The mirrors were framed with white roses made of seashells. From the ceiling hung enormous glass chandeliers, blue icicle bushes shedding teardrops of blue glass light on the gold furniture."

Anais Nin

Through research and experimentation I wish to skirt the margins of different genres, cultural styles and social codes, by incorporating and exploring sculptural and painterly processes into jewellery making practice.

My research aims to investigate the history, symbolism and evolution of representations of the human face in the Modern and Post Modern period. It attempts to reconfigure the meaning of the portrait of faces through an examination of the language of figuration, the industrial technique of electroforming and enamel in jewellery making practice. I investigate the possibilities in the imaginings of the human face.

Trina 2010
neckpiece
copper, silk, fresh water pearls, enamel, paint, lace,
electroformed, silver plate
420 x 250 x 15 mm

Anais 2008
brooch
wax, lace, synthetic pearls, copper, acrylic,
paint, found object, 9ct rose gold
90 x 80 15 mm

renee ugazio

de-phile *"A file works by persuasion; it reduces the force of assault instead of intensifying it. In place of one strong jab, it resorts to a host of weak prods, one after the other, which attack in an orderly fashion like an army of ants."* [8]

Almost every act of jewellery making is punctuated with filing; it is a process of wearing away, removing, coercing; it is multiple and recurrent. *De-phile* transforms our understanding of a file by relocating it from the brutal context of the workshop to the highly sensitive and responsive site of the body giving jewellery a gesture of emotional connectedness. It seems paradoxical that these symbolic gestures reflect little of the compromise and friction that is apparent and productive in many relationships. *De-phile* also uses the poetics of the file as a tool of coercion or persuasion to reflect on how jewellery is often used to that end. In the wearing of these works one is subject to an ongoing, but inoffensive friction.

De-phile references classic forms in jewellery with loaded meaning: engagement rings, wedding bands, shackles, cuffs. It is not unintentional that the gems (symbolically the thing to which we ascribe value) are tension set.

De- Phile demonstrates how jewellery objects can reflect the intended use of a file whilst having a poetic relationship with the body of the wearer. This work addresses the topos of wearing and making and how the two are inextricably linked.

De-Phile 2009
ring
steel, diamond
24 x 24 x 9 mm

8 Morábito, Fabio, Toolbox, Bloomsbury Publishing, London, 1999

De-Phile 2009
cuffs
steel, citrine
75 x 75 x 23 mm

linda hughes

recontextualising the cautionary sign

The 'Stripe'; historically favoured as a **metonym** for danger, exclusion, and as a device used to attract attention, is exploited in a novel context. Street signage is manipulated in shape, colour, texture and pattern. Bringing familiar motifs into a jewellery context re-examines the subject, shifting the iconography into fiction.

Cautionary street signage is designed to scream its presence; it is rich and compelling in the landscape yet with familiarity can remain invisible amid the sheer everydayness of the streetscape. Lifting familiar motifs into a jewellery context re examines the subject, shifting the iconography into fiction and may only tenuously be connected to the original.

It's important to me to have a reaction to my work when it's worn or displayed, from the maker, the wearer, to the audience. In a quotation attributed to Marcel Duchamp, he suggests: "... the creative act is not performed by the artist alone; the spectator brings the work in contact with the external world by deciphering and interpreting its inner qualifications and thus adds his contribution to the creative act."

Stop the traffic, wearable pieces reflect the complex theatre of public space.

With an interest in composition, I look closely at a piece of jewellery; I seek a formula or convention and observe, if I'm lucky, how the maker has mastered and then experimented with the work. The 17th-century Chinese scholar Ji Cheng had a design principle of 'hide and reveal' where the view was obscured, but enticing, then revealing elements of surprise.

Quiet restraint is elusive and my work shouts, 'Look at me!'

Flight Brooch 2010
laminate, acrylic, silver, steel
90 x 165 x 10 mm

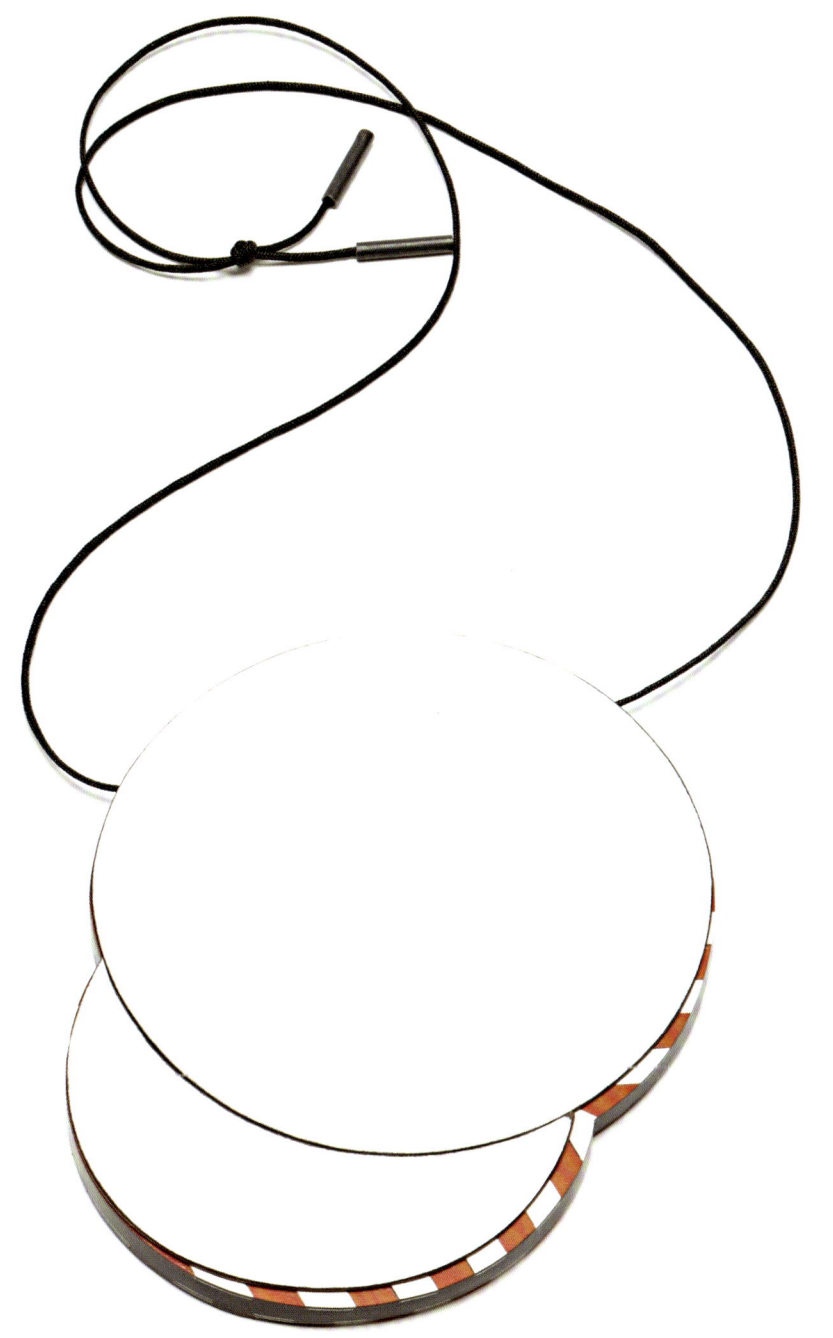

Black & Red & White Sub 1 2010
necklace
laminate, acrylic, silver, silk
95 x 95 x 30 mm

christopher earl milbourne

fusion: anarchy and architecture

Fusion is the phenomenon upon which my art practice is built. The process can be defined by the heating of objects constructed of sterling silver until they join together. The plight of the material under the duress of prolonged exposure to heat is evident in the varied surfaces and remains, warped, melted, deformed or unscathed. An exposed wire caught out in the flame might retreat into a ball, and drop and splatter insignificantly onto a substrate or wall, smeared and forgotten. A vertical wall may resemble paper, folding gracefully and resting a corner onto itself to form a perfect arc, or miserably dissolve from existence entirely. Through fusion the walls and substrates shimmer incandescently, the temperatures of their mass quickly approaching melting point. This shimmering informs the 'fuser' that the time is right for the joining of components to occur. I choose to fuse architectural forms, which seems to highlight the many nuances and tricky mood swings that the flame employs. A structure built skyward is humbled by fire, and must resume its heaven-bound quest without hesitation. The phoenix cities dissolve and are reborn, crippled and disfigured, bearing the scars of their initiation. The individual pieces symbolise a microcosm or microenvironment. They are not place- or time-specific, but more-so future ruins of an empire that never existed. It is for the viewer or wearer to place the judgement of where when and who resided within the defeated walls and under the collapsed roofs of these unglorified remains.

Exterior Wall Section [EWS]
Developed by Trinity Bridge Construction Co 2010
brooch with stand
sterling silver, stainless steel
110 x 110 x 60 mm

Megasilo with Overbearing Management Quarters 2010
brooch with stand
sterling silver, monel, enamel, stainless steel
160 x 105 x 70 mm

nicole polentas

Jewellery objects can initiate an engagement with and understanding of cultural place, re-creating the diachronic characteristics of the Cretan urban landscape. The objects are a materialisation of the improvised folk songs known as *Amanes, Mandinades*, and *The Rizitiko*. They examine the transcultural evolution between East and West, constructing narratives of cultural identity. They encapsulate language as a foundation of form, projecting the false utopia and bereavement of old and new civilisations, challenging the socio-political preconceptions of symbolic place. The objects are constructed within the framework of the *Karagiozis* character. As the main protagonist in urban theatre, *Karagiozis* is a powerful symbol in itself, in contemporary Greece, even to the Greeks of diaspora, as a popularised archetype and political expression of the common man. *Karagiozis* draws on the cultural identities explored in the urban theatre to negotiate and define boundaries and sense of place within the community.

The jewellery objects establish a period and locale, set within an unfastened social framework as opposed to a fixed historological perspective, which empowers the viewer to determine a personal assimilation of truth. Through the path of history, a distortion occurs by which notable heroes or characters are chosen whose ambitions and actions depict the desires of the people to integrate into the established ideal of the standard reality.

The objects both exemplify and distort fragments of history embedded in the landscape, and embodied within the layers of time and place.

The Fountain of the Pasha 2010
brooch
sterling silver, photo, plastic, glass powder,
paint, stainless steel
120 x 100 x 55 mm

O' Karagöz (is), Belalis 2010
neckpiece
sterling silver, copper, photo, image, plastic,
glass powder, paint
510 x 220 x 55 mm

artist
biographies

Anita Van Doorn

**Bachelor of Arts (Fine Art),
Gold and Silversmithing RMIT University, 2007
Bachelor of Arts (Fine Art) Honours,
Gold and Silversmithing RMIT University, 2010**

Significant Group Exhibitions

2008 *Small Beautiful Objects*, Self Preservation Gallery, Melbourne

2008 *Talente 2008,* Internationale Handwerksmesse, Munich

2008, 2009 *It's Got Legs*, Gold and Silversmithing Postgraduate and Alumni Award Exhibition, RMIT School of Art Gallery, Melbourne

2008 *International Graduation Show 2008,* Galerie Marzee, Nijmegen

2011 *Jewellery Topos*, Galerie Marzee, Nijmegen, , Gallery Loupe, Montclair, New Jersey

Significant Prizes and Awards

2007 Debbie Sheezel Award for Conceptual Design

2007 Siemens Fine Art Scholarship recipient

2010 New Work Emerging Artist Grant, Australia Council for the Arts

Publications

Anita van Doorn, *The Meaning in Making*, RMIT Gold and Silversmithing Graduate Exhibition catalogue, RMIT University Press, 2007.

Vanessa Paech (ed.), Artist Profile on Anita van Doorn, Arts Hub Australia (website), January 7 2008.

Le Van, M. (ed.), *500 Enameled Objects; A Celebration of Color on Metal*, Lark Books Sterling Publishing, New York, 2009

Christopher Earl Milbourne

Bachelor of Arts (Fine Art), Gold and Silversmithing RMIT University, 2007

Master of Fine Arts, Gold and Silversmithing RMIT University, 2009

Significant Group Exhibitions

2007 50 Brooches, CQ Gallery, Arts Queensland, Brisbane

2008 W.E. McMillan Collection: Selected Gold and Silversmithing 1961- 2007, Project Space, Melbourne

2008 Object- New Design, Object Gallery, Sydney, NSW, Melbourne Museum, Melbourne

2009 Melbourne Hollowware, Galerie Marzee, Nijmegen, RMIT School of Art Gallery, Melbourne

2010 By Example, Museum of Arts and Crafts, Itami, Japan

2010 Treasure Room – Australia, Galerie Handwerk, Munich

2010 International Graduation Show 2010, Galerie Marzee, Nijmegen

2011 Jewellery Topos, Gallery Loupe, Montclair, New Jersey

Significant Prizes and Awards

2007 Don Begbie Award for excellence in Gold and Silversmithing, RMIT University

2008 Commonwealth Supported Place

Publications

Galerie Marzee, Marzee Magazine #66, Nijmegen, 2009

Baines R., Melbourne Hollowware, School of Art, RMIT University, Gold and Silversmithing, 2009

Baines R., Treasure Room – Australia/Schatzkammer – Australein, Australian Scholarly Publishing, Melbourne, 2009

Sydney College of the Arts, By example: Australian Contemporary Jewellery, Museum of Arts and Craft- ITAMI, 2010

Le Van M (ed.), 500 Silver Jewelry Designs, Lark Books USA, 2011

Works in Public Collections

Block 101 Gallery, Melbourne

The W.E McMillan Collection, RMIT University, Melbourne

Significant Events

2008 Planet Furniture commission

2009 Presentation, Gerrit Rietveld Academie, Amsterdam, The Netherlands

2009 Marzee '09, Thursday Lecture Series, RMIT University

2010 Jewellery Practice as a Site for Enquiry, Symposium, RMIT, Kaleide Theatre, Melbourne

Dougal Haslem

**Bachelor of Arts (Fine Art), Gold and Silversmithing (With Distinction) RMIT University, 2007
Master of Fine Arts, Gold and Silversmithing RMIT University, 2009**

Significant Solo Exhibitions

2011 The Turtle and the Merman, Pieces of Eight, Melbourne

Significant Group Exhibitions

2008 Hatched, Perth Institute of Contemporary Art, Perth

2008 My Pet Rock, Pieces of Eight, Melbourne

2008, 2009 It's Got Legs, Gold and Silversmithing Postgraduate and Alumni Award Exhibition, RMIT School of Art Gallery, Melbourne

2008 International Graduation Show 2008, Galerie Marzee, Nijmegen

2009 – 2011 Jewellery Topos, Galerie Marzee, Nijmegen, Gallery Loupe, Montclair, New Jersey

2009 Contemporary Australian Silver and Metalwork exhibition, BUDA, Historic Home & Garden, Castlemaine

2009 RMIT University Master of Fine Art Graduate Show '09, Guilford Lane Gallery, Melbourne

2010 International Graduation Show 2010, Galerie Marzee, Nijmegen

Significant Prizes and Awards

2008 Commonwealth Supported Place

2009 Diana Morgan RMIT Postgraduate Gold and Silversmithing Second Prize, RMIT University

Publications

Hatched 08. National graduate show catalogue. PICA, 2008

Galerie Marzee (ed.), International Graduation Show 2008, Galerie Marzee, Nijmegen, 2008

Pieces of Eight Blog, Featured Artist, http://piecesofeightgallery.blogspot.com/ 2008

Galerie Marzee, Marzee Magazine #66, Nijmegen, 2009

Zilles L., Stebbins.R, Contemporary Australian Silver & Metalwork Exhibition, Buda Historic Home and Garden, Castlemaine, 2009

Significant Events

2010 Seminar, Making Objects Personal, Casey Plaza Lecture Theatre, RMIT University

Elfrun Lach

Bachelor of Arts (Fine Art), Gold and Silversmithing RMIT University, 2004
Bachelor of Arts (Fine Art) Honours, Gold and Silversmithing RMIT University, 2005
Master of Arts, Gold and Silversmithing RMIT University, 2010

Significant Solo Exhibitions

2006 Correlation, Pieces of Eight, Melbourne

Significant Group Exhibitions

2005 Marzee International Graduation Show, Galerie Marzee, Nijmegen,

2006, 2008 It's Got Legs, Gold and Silversmithing Postgraduate and Alumni Award Exhibition, RMIT School of Art Gallery, Melbourne

2007 Beyond Metal: Contemporary Australian Jewellery and Holloware (sic.), Lalit Kala Academy, Chennai and New Delhi, India; Prince of Wales Museum, Mumbai, India; Abstract Art Gallery, Bangalore, India; NN Gallery, Kuala Lumpur, Malaysia; Nanyang Academy of Fine Arts, Singapore

2007 50 Brooches, Craft Queensland, Brisbane

2008 Rowena Gough and Elfrun Lach, Museum of South Australia, Adelaide

2008 W.E. McMillan Collection: Selected Gold and Silversmithing 1961-2007, Project Space, Melbourne

2008 Beyond Metal: Contemporary Australian Jewellery and Holloware (sic.), Hamilton Art Gallery, Hamilton, Australia; RMIT Gallery, Melbourne

2009 – 2011 Jewellery Topos, Galerie Marzee, Nijmegen, Gallery Loupe, Montclair, New Jersey

Significant Prizes and Awards

2004 Nomination Wolf Wennrich Award for Gold and Silversmithing, RMIT University

2005 Emily Hope Award for Figurative Work, RMIT University

Publications

R. Baines, L. Fischer (eds.), Look, RMIT University Press, Melbourne, 2004

R. Baines, J. Wade, S. Marsland, Graduate Work, RMIT University Press, Melbourne, 2005

Galerie Marzee (ed.), International Graduation Show 2005, Galerie Marzee, Nijmegen, 2005

Elfrun Lach - Correlation Exhibition Catalogue, Pieces of Eight, Melbourne, 2006

S. Davies (ed.), Beyond Metal: Contemporary Australian Jewellery and Holloware (sic), RMIT Gallery, Melbourne, 2006

P. Asensio (ed.), Bijoux. Illustration et Design, Maomao Publications, Barcelona, 2008

A. Lim (ed.), The Compendium Finale of Contemporary Jewellers, Darling Publications, Cologne & New York, 2009

M. Serrats (ed.), Jewelry Design Handbook, booQs Publishers, Antwerp, 2010

Significant Events

2004 Nomination Wolf Wennrich Award for Gold and Silversmithing, RMIT University

2005 Emily Hope Award for Figurative Work, RMIT University

Works in Public Collections

The W.E McMillan Collection, RMIT University, Melbourne

Elfrun Lach appears courtesy of Charon Kransen Arts.

Julie Mitchell

**Bachelor of Arts (Fine Art), Gold and Silversmithing
RMIT University, 1985
Bachelor of Arts (Honours) Gold and Silversmithing
RMIT University, 1998
Master of Arts, Gold and Silversmithing
RMIT University, 2007**

Significant Solo Exhibitions

1988 Solo Exhibition in conjunction with a private collection of Bark Paintings, Emerald Hill Gallery, Melbourne

1990 Piccolo Gallery, Melbourne

2007 Yathabhuta / as it is, School of Art Gallery RMIT University, Melbourne

Significant Group Exhibitions

2000 Australian Craft and Design Showcase, Glen Eira City Gallery, Fresh Craft Victoria Multiplex Exhibition, Craft Victoria, Melbourne

2007, 2008 It's Got Legs, Gold and Silversmithing Postgraduate and Alumni Award Exhibition, RMIT School of Art Gallery, Melbourne

2009 – 2011 Jewellery Topos, Galerie Marzee, Nijmegen, the Netherlands; Gallery Loupe, Montclair

Significant Prizes and Awards

2008 Commonwealth Supported Place

2009 Diana Morgan RMIT Postgraduate Gold and Silversmithing Second Prize, RMIT University

Publications

Galerie Marzee, Marzee Magazine #66, Nijmegen, 2009

Karla Way

Bachelor of Arts (Fine Art), Gold and Silversmithing
RMIT University, 2007
Bachelor of Arts (Honours) Gold and Silversmithing
RMIT University, 2008

Significant Solo Exhibitions

2008 Terra Incognita, City Library Niches, Melbourne

Significant Group Exhibitions

2007 Filippo Raphael FRESH! Award Exhibition, Craft Victoria, Melbourne

2008 W.E. McMillan Collection: Selected Gold and Silversmithing 1961-2007, Project Space/Spare Room, Melbourne

2008 International Graduation Show 2008, Galerie Marzee, Nijmegen

2008 It's Got Legs, Gold and Silversmithing Postgraduate and Alumni Award Exhibition, RMIT School of Art Gallery, Melbourne

2008 My World Is 15x15, 374 Gallery, Melbourne

2009 – 2011 Jewellery Topos, Galerie Marzee, Nijmegen; Gallery Loupe, Montclair, New Jersey

Significant Prizes and Awards

2005 Debbie Sheezel Award for Enamelling, RMIT University

2005 Koodak Award for Top First Year Student, RMIT University

2006 Koodak Award for Top Second Year Student, RMIT University

2007 Wolf Wennrich Award for Gold and Silversmithing, RMIT University

2008 Wolf Wennrich Award for Gold and Silversmithing, RMIT University

Publications

Burns, J.B. Hot Designs of the Times, The Age, Melbourne, 2 Jan 2009

Works in Public Collections

W. E. McMillan Collection, RMIT University, Melbourne

Katherine Brunacci

**Bachelor of Arts (Fine Art), Gold and Silversmithing
RMIT University, 2007
Diploma in Gemmology, Gemmological Institute
of Australia, 2009
Practical Diamond Grading, Gemmological Institute
of Australia, 2009
Master of Fine Arts, Gold and Silversmithing
RMIT University, 2009**

Significant Group Exhibitions

2004 National Tertiary Art Prize, Powerhouse Gallery, Launceston

2004 ART Rage, Queen Victoria Museum, Melbourne

2008, 2009 It's Got Legs, Gold and Silversmithing Postgraduate and Alumni Award Exhibition, RMIT School of Art Gallery, Melbourne

2008 Marzee International Graduation Show 2007, Galerie Marzee, Nijmegen

2009 – 2011 Jewellery Topos, Galerie Marzee, Nijmegen; Gallery Loupe, Montclair, New Jersey

2009 Brink, Poemina Gallery, Launceston

2010 Gallery Fifty Four Opening, Gallery Fifty Four, Launceston

Significant Prizes and Awards

2007 RMIT Klepner Limited Series Prize in Gold and Sllversmithing, RMIT University

2008 Diana Morgan Postgraduate Award, Second Prize, RMIT University

Publications

Noise Artist of the Day, www.noise.com, 2006

Kirsten Haydon

Certificate in Contemporary Jewellery Design and
Construction, Manukau Institute of Technology, 1994
Bachelor of Arts (Fine Art), Gold and Silversmithing,
RMIT University, 1999
Master of Arts by Research, Gold and Silversmithing,
RMIT University, 2004
Doctor of Philosophy, Gold and Silversmithing,
RMIT University, 2009

Significant Solo Exhibitions

2000 – 2001 poppy's poppies, Royal Jewellery Studio and Auckland Museum, Auckland

2002 in the drawer, Craft Victoria, Melbourne; touring exhibition Auckland Museum, The Dowse, The Hawkes Bay Museum

2006 room with a view, Christchurch Art Gallery, Christchurch

2007 on the shelf, Gallery Funaki, Melbourne

2009 Ice Terrane, Objectspace, Auckland; Auckland Festival 2009 Visual Arts Programme

2009 Ice Table, Toi, Japan

Significant Group Exhibitions

2004 International Graduation Show 2004, Gallery Marzee, Nijmegen

2004 Metal Element of Four Countries, International Design Centre, Nagoya

2006 The Cicely & Colin Rigg Contemporary Design Award 2006, National Gallery of Victoria, Melbourne

2008 Schmuck 2008, Internationale Handwerksmesse, Munich; touring exhibition Birmingham City University Gallery, Birmingham, United Kingdom; Miejska Galeria Sztuki, Lodzi, Poland

2008 Sinfonia Antarctica, The New Dowse, Wellington

2009 – 2011 Jewellery Topos, Galerie Marzee, Nijmegen; Gallery Loupe, Montclair, New Jersey

2009 Four Jewellers, Melbourne Australie, Espace Solidor, Cagnes Sur Mer, France, Galerie Biró, Munich

2010 Treasure Room – Australia, Galerie Handwerk, Munich

Significant Prizes and Awards

2003 Kurt Albrecht Award for Jewellery, Ernest Leviny Commemorative Silver Exhibition, Buda Historic Home and Garden, Castlemaine

2003 Creative New Zealand Grant for Promotion and Presentation: The Promotion of New Zealand Jewellery, The Jewellers and Metalsmiths Group of Australia International Conference, RMIT University, Melbourne

2004 - 2005 Antarctic Arts Fellowship, New Zealand

2005 Thomas Gold Award, The Dowse, Wellington

2006 Teaching Award, Early Career Academic, Design and Social Context Portfolio, RMIT University, Melbourne

2007 Diana Morgan RMIT Postgraduate Gold and Silversmithing First Prize, RMIT University, Melbourne

2008 Creative New Zealand Grant for Promotion and Presentation; Participating at Schmuck international jewellery exhibition

2008 Australia Council for the Arts, New Work Established

2009 Ronnie Bauer RMIT Postgraduate Gold and Silversmithing Travelling Prize

Kirsten Haydon

Publications

Jacquard, N., 'In the Drawer: A Closer Look at a Contemporary New Zealand Jeweler,' Metalsmith Society of North American Goldsmiths, Ohio, v.24 no.5, 2004

Clement, T., 'From a Different Landscape: An Exhibition of Jewelry and Objects Responding the New Zealand Landscape,' Metalsmith, Society of North American Goldsmiths, Ohio, v.25 no.1, 2005

Baines, R., Kirsten Haydon, Artist catalogue, Kirsten Haydon and Neal Haslem, Melbourne, 2007

Devery, J., Whitfield D., and The National Gallery of Victoria. Cicely & Colin Rigg Contemporary Design Award. The Council Of Trustees Of The National Gallery Of Victoria, Melbourne, 2006

Losche, W. (ed.), Schmuck 2008 Edition Handwerk, International Handwerskmesse, Munich, 2008

Bartlett Pitt, D., 'The Éclat Of The Musée, Australians on permanent show in Paris,' The Australian Financial Review, June 2008

Le Van, M. (ed.), 500 Enameled Objects; A Celebration of Color on Metal, Lark Books Sterling Publishing, New York, 2009

Biro, O., Four Jewellers - Robert Baines, Nicholas Bastin, Simon Cottrell Kirtsen Haydon - Melbourne Australie, Espace Solidor, 2009

Findies, K. (ed.), By example: Australian Contemporary Jewellery, Itami, Japan and The University of Sydney, 2009

Damian Skinner, April 2009, Antarctic Exploration: Kirsten Haydon's Ice Terrane, http://pauadreams.co.nz/reviews/antarctic-exploration-kirsten-haydons-ice-terrane/

Baines, R. (ed.), Treasure Room Australia - Schatzkammer Australien, Australian Scholarly Publishing, 2009

Works in Public Collections

Musée des Arts Décoratifs, Paris

Antarctica New Zealand, Christchurch

Te Papa, Museum of New Zealand, Wellington

The Dowse, Wellington

RMIT Union Arts Collection, RMIT University, Melbourne

The W.E McMillan Collection, RMIT University, Melbourne

Significant Events

2002-present Lecturer, Enamelling, Gold and Silversmithing, School of Art, RMIT University, Melbourne

2004 Curator, From a Different Landscape, Horti Hall, during The Jewellers and Metalsmiths Group of Australia International Conference, RMIT University, Melbourne

2004-2005 Antarctic Arts Fellow, New Zealand

2007- Curator and Organiser, Wondernamel, Yearly RMIT Gold and Silversmithing enamelling exhibition, Melbourne

2008 Program for International Visiting Artist-in-Residence (PIVA), Henry Radford Hope School of Fine Arts, Indiana University, Bloomington, USA

2010 Acting Course Coordinator, Jewellery, Charles Sturt University, Wagga Wagga

Linda Hughes

**Bachelor of Arts (Fine Art) Honours first class,
Gold and Silversmithing, RMIT University, 2005
Master of Arts, Gold and Silversmithing,
RMIT University, current candidate**

Significant Solo Exhibitions

2009 Signwear, Craft Victoria, Melbourne

2010 Metynomy, Craft Victoria, Melbourne

2010 Metynomy, Jam Factory, Adelaide

Significant Group Exhibitions

2009 – 2011 Jewellery Topos, Galerie Marzee, Nijmegen, Gallery Loupe, Montclair, New Jersey

2010 – 2011 Contemporary Wearables '09 and Commemorative Wearables Tour, Rosny Barn Art
Gallery, Tasmania, Academy Art Gallery, School of Visual and Performing Arts, University of Tasmania,
Launceston, Manly Art Gallery & Museum, New South Wales, Logan Art Gallery, Queensland

2010 Treasure Room – Australia, Galerie Handwerk, Munich

2010 National Contemporary Jewellery Award, Griffith Regional Art Gallery, NSW

2010 HOHOHO, Workshop Bilk, ACT

Significant Prizes and Awards

2005 Toowoomba Contemporary Wearables Award

2005 The Filippo Raphael Fresh Award

2006 RMIT Postgraduate Scholarship

Publications

Le Van M. (ed), 500 Plastic Jewelry Designs, Lark Books, 2005

Le Van M. (ed), 500 Necklaces, Lark Books, 2006

Hughes L., Shared Zone, Gallery Ingot 2007

Le Van M. (ed), 500 Pendants, Lark Books, 2008

Ianni N. et al, Handmade in Melbourne, Geoff Slattery Publications 2009

Lim A. Compendium Finale of Contemporary Jewellers 2008. Darling Publications, 2009, Germany
Melbourne Design Guide, Alphabet Press, Melbourne 2009

Audio Design Museum, Melbourne, Vic. Aust. 2010,

Baines R., Treasure Room – Australia/Schatzkammer – Australein, Australian Scholarly Publishing,
Melbourne, 2009

Works in Public Collections

Powerhouse Museum, Sydney

Musée des Arts Décoratifs,
Paris

Art Gallery of South Australia,
Adelaide

Toowoomba Regional Art
Gallery, Toowoomba

Linda Hughes appears courtesy
of Charon Kransen Arts.

Significant Events

2009 Lecture, Art Forum,
Australian National University,
Canberra, ACT

2009 Lecture, BIAD
(Birmingham Inst. of Art &
Design) Birmingham, UK

2010 Craft Victoria Exhibition
Advisory Panel, Melbourne

Lucy Hearn

Bachelor of Arts (Fine Art), Gold and Silversmithing, RMIT University, 2006
Master of Fine Arts, Gold and Silversmithing, RMIT University, 2008

Significant Solo Exhibitions

2008 Lucy Hearn, Encounter, Craft Victoria, Melbourne

Significant Group Exhibitions

2007 Talente 2007, Internationale Handwerksmesse, Munich

2007, 2009 Contemporary Australian Silver and Metalwork exhibition, BUDA, Historic Home & Garden, Castlemaine

2007, 2008, 2009 It's Got Legs, Gold and Silversmithing Postgraduate and Alumni Award Exhibition, RMIT School of Art Gallery, Melbourne

2008 W.E. McMillan Collection: Selected Gold and Silversmithing 1961-2007, Project Space/Spare Room, Melbourne

2008 Small Beautiful Objects Awards, Self Preservation, Melbourne

2008 Transformation, Gallery Funaki International Jewellery Award 2008, Gallery Funaki, Melbourne

2008 In The Making, Craft Victoria Professional Members Exhibition, Craft Victoria, Melbourne

2009 – 2011 Jewellery Topos, Galerie Marzee, Nijmegen; First Site Gallery, Melbourne; Gallery Loupe, Montclair, New Jersey

Significant Prizes and Awards

2005 Ernst Fries Silversmithing Award, Special Commendation, RMIT University, Melbourne

2006 Kathlyn Harris Fashion Jewellery Award, RMIT University, Melbourne

2007 Diana Morgan RMIT Postgraduate Gold and Silversmithing Second Prize, RMIT University, Melbourne

2008 e. g. etal Design Award, Melbourne

Publications

Talente 2008, Handwerkskammer fur Munchen und Oberbayern, Munich, 2007

Lim, A. The Compendium Finale of Contemporary Jewellers 2008, Darling Publications, Cologne and New York, 2009

Stappmanns, V. (Ed), The Melbourne Design Guide, Alphabet Press, Melbourne, 2009

Works in Public Collections

W.E McMillan Collection, RMIT University, Melbourne

Mel Miller

**Bachelor of Fine Arts (Metalsmithing),
Arizona State University, 2004
Master of Arts (Fine Art), Gold and Silversmithing,
RMIT University, 2009**

Significant Solo Exhibitions

2009 Metamemorphosis, Off the Kerb Gallery, Melbourne

2009 Persuasions of Memory, RMIT School of Art Gallery, Melbourne

Significant Group Exhibitions

2001 Chasing the Space, Harry Wood Gallery, Tempe, Arizona

2002 Sawdust and Filings, Harry Wood Gallery, Tempe, Arizona

2008, 2009 It's Got Legs, Gold and Silversmithing Postgraduate and Alumni Award Exhibition, RMIT School of Art Gallery, Melbourne

2008 National Contemporary Jewellery Award Exhibition, Griffith

2009 Contemporary Australian Silver and Metalwork exhibition, BUDA, Historic Home & Garden, Castlemaine

2009 – 2011 Jewellery Topos, Galerie Marzee, Nijmegen; Gallery Loupe, Montclair, New Jersey

2010 - 2011 New Traditional Jewellery, Sieraad International Jewellery Art Fair, Amsterdam; der villa Bengel, Idar Oberstein, Germany; Museum for Modern Arts in Arnhem, Arnhem

2010 Talente 2010, Internationale Handwerksmesse, Munich

Significant Prizes and Awards

2003 Arizona State University Herberger College of Fine Arts Scholarship

2008 Small Beautiful Objects Award, Melbourne

Publications

Le Van, M. (ed.), 500 Enameled Objects; A Celebration of Color on Metal, Lark Books Sterling Publishing, New York, 2009

Galerie Marzee, Marzee Magazine #66, Nijmegen, 2009

Talente 2011, Handwerkskammer fur Munchen und Oberbayern, Munich, 2011

Significant Events

2007 Public Lecture, Making Personal Object Seminar, RMIT Storey Hall

2009 Lecture, Lunchtime Lecture Series, RMIT University, Melbourne

2009 Public Lecture, Gerrit Rietveld Academie, Amsterdam

2009 Assistant Lecturer – Jewellery, RMIT University, Melbourne

2009– Teacher – Jewellery, North Melbourne Institute of TAFE, Melbourne

2010 Master of Fine Arts Examination Assessor, RMIT University, Melbourne

Natalia Milosz-Piekarska

Bachelor of Arts, Design/Visual Communication, Monash University, 2001
Certificate Applied Arts/Jewellery Design, CAE Melbourne, 2004
Bachelor of Arts (Fine Art), Gold and Silversmithing RMIT University, 2007
Bachelor of Arts (Honours, First class) Gold and Silversmithing, RMIT University, 2008

Significant Solo Exhibitions

2008 The Passenger, Craft Victoria, Encounter Window. Melbourne

2010 Bad Beast Do Not Harm Me, (joint show), Craft Victoria, Melbourne

Significant Group Exhibitions

2007 The Filippo Raphael Fresh! Awards, Craft Victoria, Melbourne

2007 Fresh Crop, National Design Centre Gallery, Melbourne

2008 It's Got Legs, Gold and Silversmithing Postgraduate and Alumni Award Exhibition, RMIT School of Art Gallery, Melbourne

2009 – 2011 Jewellery Topos, Galerie Marzee, Nijmegen, First Site Gallery, Melbourne, Gallery Loupe, Montclair, New Jersey

2009 Precious Pendants, Object Gallery, Sydney

2010 Re:Production. Keeper Gallery at Gaffa, Sydney

2011 Talente 2011, Internationale Handwerksmesse, Munich

Significant Prizes and Awards

2006 Ernst Fries Award for Excellence in Silversmithing, RMIT University

2006 'Innovation and best execution' prize, Nu Arte. Melbourne

2007 Filippo Raphael FRESH! Awards, Craft Victoria Mentorship Award, Melbourne

2007 Katheryn Harris Fashion Award, Jewellery, RMIT University

2008 Emily Hope Prize for figurative work, Jewellery, RMIT University

2009 ArtStart Grant, Australian Arts Council, Sydney

2010 British Council, 'Realise Your Dream' Award, Sydney

Publications

Le Van, M. (ed.), 500 Enameled Objects; A Celebration of Color on Metal, Lark Books Sterling Publishing, New York, 2009

Galerie Marzee, Marzee Magazine #66, Nijmegen, 2009

Talente 2011, Handwerkskammer fur Munchen und Oberbayern, Munich, 2011

Works in Public Collections

The W.E McMillan Collection, RMIT University, Melbourne

Significant Events

2006 SOYA (Spirit of Youth Awards), finalist for Jewellery Design, Melbourne

2008 Finalist 'Siemens Fine Art Scholarship', Melbourne

2008 E.g. Etal 10 Year Anniversary Pendant Competition, Finalist, Melbourne

2010 The Social Studio, Volunteer jewellery skills teacher to young refugee community, Melbourne

2010 Pieces of Eight, Gallery assistant, Melbourne

2010 Small Object Ideation', Lecturer, Gold and Silversmithing, RMIT University, Melbourne

Nicholas Bastin

Bachelor of Arts (Fine Art), Gold and Silversmithing, RMIT University, 1989
Bachelor of Arts, (Fine Arts - Honours, First Class), Gold and Silversmithing, RMIT University 1993
Master of Arts (Fine Arts), Gold and Silversmithing, RMIT University, 2004
Doctor of Philosophy, Gold and Silversmithing, RMIT University, current candidate

Significant Solo Exhibitions

2002 Battle of the Drones, Mezzanine Gallery, Ivy Hopes, Melbourne

2006 Asakusa Window, Object Gallery, Sydney

2007 Dangerous Shell, Glitzern, Melbourne

Significant Group Exhibitions

2005 International Graduation Show 2005, Galerie Marzee, Nijmegen

2006 Cicely & Colin Rigg Award Contemporary Design Award, Ian Potter Centre, National Gallery of Victoria, Melbourne

2007 Beyond Metal: Contemporary Australian Jewellery and Holloware, India and Singapore

2009 – 2011 Jewellery Topos, Galerie Marzee, Nijmegen, the Netherlands; Gallery Loupe, Montclair

2009 Melbourne Hollow Ware, Gallery Marzee, Nijmegen

2009 Four Jewellers, Melbourne Australie, Espace Solidor, Cagnes Sur Mer, France, Galerie Biró, Munich

2010 By Example, Australian Contemporary Jewellery, The Museum of Arts & Crafts Itami, Itami, Japan

2010 Treasure Room – Australia, Galerie Handwerk, Munich

Significant Prizes and Awards

1993 Emily Hope Figurative Award, RMIT University

1995 Australia Council for the Arts Grant, Traineeship with Metalsmith Mark Edgoose

2003 Sapphex/Affiliated Award for Souvenir exhibition

2004 Siemens RMIT Fine Arts Scholarship, RMIT University

2004 Diana Morgan Postgraduate Gold & Silversmithing Prize, RMIT University

2004 Australia Council for the Arts, Skills and Arts Development Grant Tokyo Studio Residency

2007 RMIT PhD Scholarship, RMIT University, Melbourne

2007 Ronnie Bauer RMIT Postgraduate Gold & Silversmithing Travelling Prize, RMIT University

Nicholas Bastin

Publications

Mc Millan, K., and Jirasek, I., Double Take. Recycling in Contemporary Craft, Craftwest Centre for Contemporary Craft, Perth, 2001

Waite, D., RMIT University School of Art Postgraduate 2005, RMIT University Press, Melbourne, 2005

Devery, J., and Whitfield, D., The Cicely & Colin Rigg Contemporary Design Award, National Gallery of Victoria, Melbourne, 2006

Davies, S., Beyond Metal: Contemporary Australian Jewellery and Holloware, RMIT Gallery, Melbourne, 2006

O'Connell, S., Fuse, Artists and Jewelers Exploring Self and Society through Diverse Technologies, Jam Factory Contemporary Craft and Design, Adelaide, 2008

Baines, Professor Dr. R., Melbourne Hollow Ware, School of Art, RMIT University Gold and Silversmithing, Melbourne, 2009

Lim, Andy, The Compendium Finale of Contemporary Jewellers 2008, Darling Publications, Cologne and New York, 2009

Zobel-Biró, Olga, Four Jewellers: Robert Baines, Nicholas Bastin, Simon Cottrell, Kirsten Haydon, Melbourne, Australie, Espace Solidor, Ville de Cagnes-sur-mer, Cagnes-sur-mer, France, 2009

Baines, Professor. Dr. R., Treasure Room – Australia/Schatzkammer – Australien, Australian scholarly Publishing Pty. Ltd. Victoria, 2009

Findeis, Dr. K., By Example, Australian Contemporary Jewellery, The Museum of Arts & Crafts Itami, Itami, Sydney College of the Arts, University of Sydney, 2010

Works in Public Collections

The W.E McMillan Collection, RMIT University, Melbourne

Ville de Cagnes-sur-Mer, France

Nicholas Bastin appears courtesy of Charon Kransen Arts.

Significant Events

1993 – 1996 Lecturer, Jewellery and Metal, Peninsula School of Art, Monash University, Frankston

1996 – 2001 Lecturer, Gold and Silversmithing, School of Art, RMIT University, Melbourne

2002 - 2006 Lecturer, Jewellery & Object Design, Sydney College of the Arts, University of Sydney

2004 Guest Speaker, Design Institute of Australia, Queensland Chapter, Brisbane

2005 Guest Speaker, Annual Public Lecture, Jewellers and Metalsmiths Group of Australia (JMGA)

2007 Guest Speaker, Beyond Metal, Singapore Design Festival, Singapore

2007 - 2010 Lecturer, Gold & Silversmithing, School of Art, RMIT University, Melbourne

Nicole Polentas

Diploma of Arts, Product Design and Jewellery, NMIT TAFE, 2003
Bachelor of Arts (Fine Art), Gold and Silversmithing (With Distinction) RMIT University, 2006
Master of Fine Arts, Gold and Silversmithing RMIT University, 2008
Doctor of Philosophy, Gold and Silversmithing RMIT University, Current Candidate

Significant Solo Exhibitions

2010 XA-O-S, The Hellenic Museum, Melbourne

Significant Group Exhibitions

2007 50 Brooches, CQ Gallery, Arts Queensland, Brisbane

2007 International Graduation Show 2007, Galerie Marzee, Nijmegen

2008 W.E McMillan Collection: Selected Gold and Silversmithing 1961- 2007, Project Space, Melbourne

2008 Talente 2008, Internationale Handwerksmesse, Munich

2009 – 2011 Jewellery Topos, Galerie Marzee, Nijmegen, Gallery Loupe, Montclair, New Jersey

2009 Contemporary Wearables '09, Toowoomba Regional Art Gallery, Queensland

2010 Treasure Room – Australia, Galerie Handwerk, Munich

2010 Thinking Through Practice – Art and Design as Research, Institute of Contemporary Arts, LaSalle College of the Arts, Singapore

Significant Prizes and Awards

2006 Don Begbie Award for excellence in Gold and Silversmithing, RMIT University

2007 Commonwealth Supported Place

2008 Kraft Design Award & Scholarship

2008 Diana Morgan RMIT Postgraduate Gold and Silversmithing First Prize, RMIT University

2009 Contemporary Wearables '09, Biennial Jewellery Award, Second Prize

2009 Australian Postgraduate Award

Publications

Galerie Marzee (ed.), International Graduation Show 2007, Galerie Marzee, Nijmegen, 2007

Talente 2008, Handwerkskammer fur Munchen und Oberbayern, Munich, 2008

Galerie Marzee, Marzee Magazine #66, Nijmegen, 2009

Zilles L., Stebbins.R, Contemporary Australian Silver & Metalwork Exhibition, Buda Historic Home and Garden, Castlemaine, 2009

Le Van M (ed.), 500 Plastic Jewelry Designs, Lark Books USA, 2009

Baines R., Treasure Room – Australia/Schatzkammer – Australein, Australian Scholarly Publishing, Melbourne, 2009

Le Van M (ed.), 500 Silver Jewelry Designs, Lark Books USA, 2011

Works in Public Collections

The W.E MacMillan Collection, RMIT University, Melbourne
Toowoomba Regional Art Gallery, Queensland

Significant Events

2007 RMIT Founders Day pin commission

2008 Gold billionth jar, Kraft commission

2009 – 2011 Exhibition manager, Jewellery Topos

2009 Presentation, Gerrit Rietveld Academie, Amsterdam, The Netherlands

2009 Marzee '09, Thursday Lecture Series, RMIT University

2009 – 2010, Administration, Treasure Room – Australia exhibition

2010 Hellenic Foundation for Culture support of XAOS exhibition

2010 'The Cretans always liars' public lecture, Hellenic Museum, Melbourne

2010 Jewellery Practice as a Site for Enquiry, Symposium, RMIT, Kaleide Theatre, Melbourne

Nina Oikawa

Bachelor of Applied Art (Metal and Jewellery), Monash University, 2003
Bachelor of Fine Art (Honours) (Metal and Jewellery), Monash University, 2004
Master of Fine Arts, Gold and Silversmithing RMIT University, 2005
Doctor of Fine Arts, Gold and Silversmithing RMIT University, Current Candidate

Significant Solo Exhibitions

2006 Fossil Jewels, Encounter, Craft Victoria, Melbourne
2006 Fossil Jewels, RMIT University First Site Gallery, Melbourne
2007 Sweet Dominance Pieces of Eight, Melbourne
2008 Wild Breeze Pablo Fanque, Sydney

Significant Group Exhibitions

2006, 2007,2008, 2009 It's Got Legs, Gold and Silversmithing Postgraduate and Alumni Award Exhibition, RMIT School of Art Gallery, Melbourne
2006 SIERAAD International Jewellery & Silver Design Fair, Amsterdam
2006 International Graduation Show 2007, Galerie Marzee, Nijmegen
2007 Talente 2007, Internationale Handwerksmesse, Munich
2007 Atelier Ravary, Galerie Marzee, Nijmegen
2008 Innovative Contemporary Jewellery, SOFA Chicago Art Fair, New York
2009 – 2011 Jewellery Topos, Galerie Marzee, Nijmegen; Gallery Loupe, Montclair, USA
2010 Treasure Room – Australia, Galerie Handwerk, Munich

Significant Prizes and Awards

2006 Galerie Marzee International Graduate Exhibition Prize, Nijmegen
2008 Diana Morgan RMIT Postgraduate Gold and Silversmithing Second Prize, RMIT University
2008 Springboard Entrepreneurship for Designers Scholarship

Publications

Sweet Dominance, The Age, Melbourne, 10 November 2007
Maddox, S. ABC Sunday Arts Program, television program, Melbourne, 6 April 2008
Press, C. (ed). All That Glitzerns, Vogue Australia, September 2008
Asensio, P. (ed.), Bijoux: Illustration et Design, Maomao Publications, Barcelona, 2008

Works in Public Collections

Gallerie Marzee, Nijmegen

Significant Events

2007 Atelier Ravary with Gallery Marzee, Belgium
2008 Springboard Entrepreneurship for Designers Program, Melbourne
2008 Guest speaker, Craft as a Career 2008, Craft Victoria, Melbourne
2010 Guest speaker, Making Object Personal, RMIT School of Art, Design Research Institute and Craft Victoria, Melbourne

Penelope Joy Pollard

Jewellery Engineering Associate Diploma, NMIT TAFE, 2002
Bachelor of Arts (Fine Art), Gold and Silversmithing (Honours) RMIT University, 2008
Master of Fine Arts by Research, Monash University, Current Candidate

Significant Group Exhibitions

2008 W.E McMillan Collection: Selected Gold and Silversmithing 1961- 2007, Project Space, Melbourne

2008, 2009 It's Got Legs, Gold and Silversmithing Postgraduate and Alumni Award Exhibition, RMIT School of Art Gallery, Melbourne

2008 International Graduation Show 2008, Galerie Marzee, Nijmegen

2009 Linden Postcard Show, Linden Gallery, Melbourne

2009 – 2011 Jewellery Topos, Galerie Marzee, Nijmegen, First Site Gallery, Melbourne, Gallery Loupe, Montclair, New Jersey

2009 Explorations 09, Gaffa Gallery, Sydney, Guilford Gallery, Melbourne

2009 Contemporary Australian Silver and Metalwork exhibition, BUDA, Historic Home & Garden, Castlemaine

2010 Graduate Metal,12 Nation Survey and Exhibition of graduates from Australia, Asia and South Africa Gallery Central Central Institute of Technology Northbridge Perth

Significant Prizes and Awards

2002 Opal Jewellery Design Awards Association, First Prize in Brooch Category

2007 Top student in Graduating class, Koodak Award for Highest Academic Achievement in Third Year, RMIT University

2006-2008 Commonwealth Learning Scholarship 2007 Emily Hope Award for Figurative work, RMIT University

2008 Emily Hope Award for Figurative work, RMIT University

2008 Commonwealth Equity Place

Publications

Edgoose M., Topos Nochos, Graduate Book, RMIT University Gold and Silversmithing, Penelope Pollard, 'Art concept of the uncanny. The disruptive potential of art explored through the psychoanalytical concept of the uncanny.' In Topos Nochos, RMIT Gold and Silversmithing Graduate Exhibition catalogue, RMIT University Press, 2007

Galerie Marzee, Marzee Magazine #66, Nijmegen, 2009

Crafts Arts International Magazine, 2007 (image only).

Pollard P., 'Objet Trouve'. In Ten Thousand Hours, RMIT University Gold and Silversmithing Graduate Exhibition catalogue, RMIT University Press, 2008.

Works in Public Collections

The W.E McMillan Collection, RMIT University, Melbourne

Renee Ugazio

Bachelor of Arts (Fine Art), Gold and Silversmithing, RMIT University, 2003
Master of Fine Arts, Gold and Silversmithing, RMIT University, 2008
Doctor of Philosophy, Gold and Silversmithing, RMIT University, current candidate

Significant Group Exhibitions

2007, 2008, 2009 It's Got Legs, Gold and Silversmithing Postgraduate and Alumni Award Exhibition, RMIT School of Art Gallery, Melbourne

2007 Luminous, Fashion & Textiles Event, First Site Gallery, Melbourne

2007 August Festival, RMIT University Brunswick Campus, Melbourne

2008 37th Parallel, First Site Gallery, Melbourne

2008 Objects in Space, Craft Victoria, Melbourne

2009 – 2011 Jewellery Topos, Galerie Marzee, Nijmegen; Gallery Loupe, Montclair, New Jersey

2010 Little Weeds: small acts of tenderness and violence, Adelaide Fringe, touring exhibition, Adelaide

2010 Signs of Change, Form, Perth

Significant Prizes and Awards

2007 August Festival, RMIT Union Arts, Conceptual Strength

2008 Master of Fine Arts Award, RMIT University

Publications

AD ASTRA PER ASPERA, City Museum at Old Treasury, Melbourne, 2003

Ugazio, R., Finding the Body, Inside Out, Jewellers' and Metalsmiths' Guild of Australia (JMGA) Conference, Adelaide, 2008

Ugazio, R. (sub-editor), Ten Thousand Hours, 2008 Graduate Catalogue RMIT Gold and Silversmithing, Melbourne, 2008

Galerie Marzee, Marzee Magazine #66, Nijmegen, 2009

Ugazio., R., two hundred and eleven, Natalie Mc Quade: eighty-seven, Trocadero ARI, Melbourne, 2009

Ugazio, R., Thresholds of five or more, Natalie Mc Quade: Five, plus and minus, Kings ARI, Melbourne, 2010

Significant events

2008 Artist in Residence, Craft Victoria, Melbourne

2008 Speaker, Finding the Body, Inside Out Jewellers' and Metalsmiths' Guild of Australia (JMGA) Conference, Adelaide

2009 Studio Theory Lecturer, RMIT University Gold and Silversmithing, Melbourne

2010 Speaker, bound and unbound, Jewellery Practice as a Site for Enquiry, Melbourne

2010 Speaker, Impolite Craft, Making Objects Personal, Melbourne

Robert Baines

**Diploma of Art, Gold and Silversmithing,
RMIT University, 1970
Master of Arts in Classics and Archaeology,
Monash University, 1998
Doctor of Philosophy, Gold and Silversmithing,
RMIT University, 2006**

Significant Solo Exhibitions

1977 Sculpture, Jewellery and Other Objects, Realities Gallery, Melbourne

1981 A Visible Likeness... Robin Gibson, Sydney; Georges Gallery, Melbourne

1982 Misteri Antipoidei, Via Veneto 50, Rome

1992-3 Robert Baines: The Art of the Goldsmith, Touring exhibition in New Zealand: Auckland Museum; Hawkes Bay Museum, Napier; Wairarapa Arts Foundation, Masterton; Suter Art Gallery, Nelson; McDougall Art Gallery, Christchurch

2004 Robert Baines Entdecker der antiken Goldschmiedetechnik, Staatliche Antikensammlungen, München

2008-9 The Schatzkammer: A Treasury of Evidence. Touring Exhibition, DESIGNMUSEO Helsinki; Museum für Angewandte Kunst Frankfurt

2010 Robert Baines: Metal, Living Treasures: Masters of Australian Craft, Object Gallery, Sydney

Significant Group Exhibitions

1980 Objects to Human Scale organised by Australia council, toured Japan, Hong Kong, Phillipines

1982 Tendenzen 1982, Schmuckmuseum, Pforzeim, West Germany

1997 Contemporary Vessels and Jewels, Australian Fine Metalwork, Shanghai Museum

1998 Brooching it Diplomatically : A Tribute to Madeleine K. Albright, Helen Drutt, Philadelphia;.The Museum of Contemporary Art, 's-Hertogenbosch, The Netherlands; Konstindustrrimuset, Helsinki; Kunstgwerbemuseum, Berlin; Schmuckmuseum, Pforzheim

1999 Contemporary Australian Craft: A Japanese View, Hokkaido Museum of Modern Art, Takaoka City Art Museum, Museum of Modern Art Shiga, Customs House Sydney

2000 Australia and Germany 8, Craft Triennale, Museum für Kunsthandwerk, Frankfurt, Art Gallery of South Australia, Object Galleries, Sydney

2005 Closer, Interventions from the MNAA Colleccions. Museu Nacional de Arte Antiga, Lisboa Portugal

2007 Field of Vision: Contemporary Jewelry and Hollowware Indiana University School of Fine Arts (SoFA) Bloomington Indiana, USA

Robert Baines

Significant Prizes and Awards

1979 Awarded a Winston Churchill Fellowship

1988 "Medibank Private Bicentennial Craft Acquisition", Australian Crafts

1992 Australia Council for the Arts Fellowship Grant

1994 Winner; Twentieth anniversary of Diamond Valley Art Award sculpture commission (National competition)

1996 Senior Fulbright Award, The Metropolitan Museum of Art (NY)

1997 Winner; Cicely and Colin Rigg Craft Award, 1997, National Gallery of Victoria

1998 Winner; The Seppelt Contemporary Art Award, Museum of Contemporary Art, Sydney

1998, 2002   Received an Andrew Mellon Conservation Fellowship at The Metropolitan Museum of Art in New York

2005 Bayerischer Staatspreis 2005 gold medal at the 57 Internationale Handwerksmesse, Munich

2007 Received research scholarship in The Sherman Fairchild Center for Objects Conservation at the Metropolitan Museum of
        Art in New York

2007 Living Treasure: Master of Australian Craft 2010

2008 Friedrich Becker Preis, Gesellschaft für Goldschmiedekunst e.V. (Association of Goldsmith's Art) Hanau Germany

Publications

Mendham D., Spiritual Values, Craft Australia, Winter 1987/2, front cover, pp.64-7

Zimmer J., Journeys of a Modern Magi, Craft Arts International, 1988 pp.49-52

Baines R. The Significance of Double Row Granulation from Palestrina Jewellery Studies 5, Society of Jewellery Historians, London,1992

Baines R (ed.)., Jewellery Philosophies, A series of seminars, JMGV, Melbourne, 1992.

Baines R., Technical Decisions in the Gold Cylinders from Praeneste", Outils et Ateliers D'Orfevres 5000-1600 AD, Musee des Antiquites
Nationales Saint-Germain-en- Laye, France, 1993

Nelson R., Robert Baines and the Deconstruction of Masculinity, Craft Victoria, Vol. 23, No. 220, 1993

Baines R., Technical Antecedents of Early Hellenistic Disc and Pendant Ear Ornaments, The Art of the Greek Goldsmith, D. Williams (ed.),
The British Museum, 1998 pp.122-126

Baines R., Partyline RMIT University Press 2004

Baines R., Antipodean Recorder Melbourne, 1980-1981 Deutsches Blockflötenmuseum, 2004

Baines R., Bracelet'Java-la-Grande' Macmillan Art Publishing 2006

Baines R., Distraction or Destruction or just Uncovering the Cover Up", Thinking Through Practice, Elizabeth Grierson, Lesley Duxbury (Ed.),
RMIT University Press, 2007

Works in Public Collections

Musee des Arts Decoratifs, Paris, France

The Metropolitan Museum of Art, NY, USA

Schmuckmuseum, Pforzheim, Germany

Victoria and Albert Museum, London

Museum für Kunst und Gewerbe, Hamburg

Ville de Cagnes-sur-Mer, France

Deutsches Blockflötenmuseum, Fulda, Germany

Museum of Fine Arts, Houston, USA

Waikato Museum of Art and History, Hamilton, New Zealand

Waikato Polytechnic, Hamilton, New Zealand.

Galerie am Graben, Vienna, Austria

Australian National Gallery, Canberra

National Gallery of Victoria

Royal Melbourne Institute of Technology, Victoria

Prime Minister's Department, Canberra

Banyule Art Collection

The Victorian State Craft Collection, Melbourne

Art Gallery of Western Australia

Diamond Valley Art Award Collection

Art Gallery of South Australia

Powerhouse Museum, Sydney

Queensland Art Gallery

Significant Events

1975 Founder and co-convenor, Craft Workers Guild of Australia.

1980 Commenced as lecturer in Gold and silversmithing at RMIT University

1999 Coòrdinator in Gold and Silversmithing, RMIT University

1995-1998   Editor of Lemel - national journal of the Jewellers & Metalsmiths Group of Australia.

2003 Judge and selector of acquisitions, "Contemporary Wearables 2003," Toowoomba Regional Art Gallery

2002-03 Chairman, Melbourne International Mokume Symposium and Exhibition, Melbourne, RMIT University www.rmit.edu/mokume

2003 Chairman, Jewellers and Metalsmiths Group of Australia International Conference, Melbourne Feb. 13-15www.jmga.org

2007 Discussion Panel member "Is it craft? Is it art? Does it matter?" coincides with "Field of Vision: Contemporary Jewelry and Hollowware" Indiana University School of Fine Arts (SoFA) Bloomington Indiana, USA.

2007 Professor of Art, RMIT University

2008, Speaker, Symposium, A Grand Passion: Global Perspectives on Contemporary Art Jewelry, with Helen Drutt, Robin Kranitzky and Kim Overstreet, Robert Baines, Claus Bury, Smithsonian American Art Museum Renwick Gallery Washington

acknow ledge- ments

Australian Jewellery Topos: Talking About Place
© 2010 Australian Scholarly Publishing Pty Ltd
Nick Walker
Director
7 Little Lothian Street North
North Melbourne Victoria 3051
tel: 03 9329 6963
fax: 03 9329 5452
email: aspic@ozemail.com.au
ASP website: www.scholarly.info

Editors

Prof. Dr Robert Baines
Nicole Polentas
Melissa Miller

School of Art, RMIT University
124 Latrobe Street,
Melbourne, VIC. 3000
Australia
robert.baines@rmit.edu.au

Authors
Prof. Dr Elizabeth Grierson RMIT University
Prof. Dr Robert Baines RMIT University

Acknowledgements

Australian Jewellery Exhibition, Gallery Loupe, New Jersey 10 March 2011 – 3 April 2011

This book has its foundations in an invitation by Gallery Loupe, New Jersey to hold an exhibition of Australian Jewellery at USA.

Directors, Gallery Loupe
Patti Bleicher
Eileen David

Exhibition Managers, Australia:
Nicole Polentas
Melissa Miller
Nina Oikawa (Finance)

Gallery Loupe
50 Church Street
Montclair, NJ
07042 USA